How The Left Was Won

OTHER BOOKS BY RICHARD MGRDECHIAN

3000 Years

How The Left Was Won

An In-depth Analysis of the Tools and
Methodologies Used by Liberals to
Undermine Society and Disrupt the
Social Order

Richard Mgrdechian

Coventry Circle

A Division of Omniscient Books

Additional information on this work or the author may be found at:
www.howtheleftwaswon.com.

The author of this work may be reached at author@howtheleftwaswon.com.

Published in San Francisco, California by Coventry Circle, a division of Omniscient
Books.

Library of Congress Control Number: 2006905156

ISBN 0-9786423-8-4.

Printed in the United States of America.

Cover design and concept by Richard Mgrdechian. Artwork by Peter Fasolino.

"Freedom is a fragile thing and is never more than one generation away from extinction. It is not ours by inheritance; it must be fought for and defended constantly by each generation, for it comes only once to a people. Those who have known freedom and then lost it have never known it again."

Ronald Reagan

CONTENTS

INTRODUCTION

Over the course of the past twenty-five years, I've watched with both fascination and horror as liberalism has degenerated from something which could at least pass for a reasonably well-intentioned social and political ideology, into what is now nothing more than a relentlessly destructive, all-consuming cesspool of never-ending hostility and raging hatred.

As I watched this transformation, I couldn't help but ask myself how it was happening. I couldn't help but ask why so many of the people who claimed to care only about peace, love, compassion and understanding, were always so vicious, so hostile, so narrow-minded and so unforgiving. I couldn't help but ask why the same people who were so adamant about wanting justice and equality in our society, always worked so hard to oppress others. Most of all, I couldn't help but ask how the country we live in could continue to allow these same kinds of people to put more and more policies into place which clearly do nothing other than drive the society into a downward spiral that could only end when it finally collapses into a state of complete anarchy. I couldn't help but ask a lot of questions—and ask I did.

Unfortunately, one of the most frustrating experiences any

rational person could ever have is to listen to liberals try to justify their position on any sort of social or political issue. However, although their arguments usually tend to make no sense whatsoever, I eventually found that if we listen closely enough, we do find that time after time they do in fact follow a set of highly predictable patterns. *How The Left Was Won* is intended to show the reader exactly what these patterns are and—more importantly—to demonstrate how all liberal statements, arguments, positions and policies are ultimately self-destructive to them, the people they claim to be helping and to the country as a whole.

In order to achieve this goal, we first introduce a new framework in which we segment and isolate all of the familiar liberal behaviors and ideologies into the most objective and discrete elements possible so as to remove the noise and ambiguity which typically exists in other forms of political analysis. Once this framework is in place, we then go on to provide numerous examples of how liberals relentlessly employ these particular tools and methodologies to push their agenda and then discuss the resulting effects they have on our society. In most cases, we also explore a number of variations of the central theme, as well as show just what the real goal of each of these behaviors actually is.

This book assumes a reasonably strong knowledge of current events as well as a general awareness of the sort of social and cultural changes that American society has experienced over the past several decades. Furthermore, my goal is not to spend page after page arguing the particular details of any specific point of view. Rather, the goal is to provide a core set of examples of liberal actions and behaviors for the sole purpose of identifying, exposing and validating the tools and methodologies they consistently use to undermine society in the hopes that these patterns will become immediately recognizable to anyone who takes the time to read this book.

There is no doubt that not everyone will agree with my

observations or my conclusions. In particular, I fully expect that liberals will do everything they possibly can in order to detract from the insights this book may offer. That being said, regardless of any personal attacks against me, the best way to confirm the validity and the pervasiveness of these tools and methodologies is to just sit back and let the liberals do the talking.

As painful as it may be, take the time to actually listen to what your liberal friends, relatives, neighbors or co-workers may say with regard to social and political issues. Listen as they speak. Listen to how they speak. Listen to the words they use and listen as they endlessly employ—consciously or unconsciously—three, four, five or more of the tools and methodologies discussed throughout this book in each and every argument they try to make.

Now do the same thing with liberal politicians, activists and members of the mainstream media. Listen to what they say and how they say it. Then take a minute to break down any of their statements, speeches or sound bites into the elements we discuss. With a little practice, it should become painfully obvious which of the particular tools or methodologies are being used at any given time as they try to justify, rationalize or defend any of their particular positions or agendas. Once you get to that point, it becomes almost too easy to tell them why they are wrong—not that I would bother though, since it is unlikely that anything anyone could do or say would ever change their mind.

In terms of structure, this book has been written as a set of individual essays, each with the express purpose of describing, explaining and exposing one specific tool or methodology regularly used by liberals. Although entire works could easily be written about any of these subjects—the concepts of Bad Competition, Groupdividual, and Relevancy and Proportion especially lend themselves to further discussion—this book does not take that approach. Rather, I have chosen to simply introduce these ideas into the public consciousness in order to provide new ways of looking at and thinking about what is happening within our society. My hope is that by showing—in no uncertain terms—exactly how liberals are undermining that society, that we may be able to take the first steps toward reversing this trend while we still can.

ONE

Promote and Exploit Divisiveness

Let's face it, when you get right down to it, all of liberalism is fueled by a singular strategy—a strategy which has been continually perfected and relentlessly executed over the past forty years. That strategy is to promote and exploit divisiveness.

Everything liberal politicians do is based on this simple principle. Tell the people that are given to hating the most, that they are the ones who are hated. Tell the people who expect the most, that they deserve more. Tell blacks to hate whites. Tell women to hate men. Tell the lazy to hate the motivated. Tell the poor that only conservatives are rich, and then be sure to tell them to hate them for it.

Class warfare, race baiting, name calling and man-hating—all with a singular goal: to get themselves in power by promoting and exploiting divisiveness. Of course, once this divisiveness turns into frenzy, these same people suddenly act as if they actually want to solve a problem that didn't even exist before they did everything they possibly could to create it.

To liberals, every issue, every situation is an opportunity to divide. History, religion, the First Amendment, the Second Amendment, the death of a soldier, a political debate, the hurricane which devastated New Orleans. Every tragedy exploited to divide. Every victory belittled to divide. Every incident, every word, every distorted statistic, every holiday—you name it, they will find some way to divide it.

Unfortunately, it's not just the politicians who promote and exploit divisiveness; it is the people as well. Malcontents, jealous of anyone with any sort of success, come up with any way they can to attack those who are more successful then they are. Someone is rich only because they stole something from them. Certain groups are more successful only because they took advantage of them. Work has nothing to do with it. Intelligence has nothing to do with it. Planning ahead has nothing to do with it. Even luck has nothing to do with it.

And what do these kinds of people view as the solution to this imaginary injustice? Why special rights, privileges and opportunities for themselves, of course. Level the playing field. Get something for nothing. Take from the rich, the white, the male dominated, homophobic society that has already given them everything. Take what they have, what they built, what they earned—whether it be money, property, liberty or opportunity—and find some way, some justification, some cause or some guise to redistribute it to the people who have done nothing to earn it. To people who refuse to compete on merit. To people who insist on taking more out of society than what they put in to it. To people who don't give a damn that their inclusion comes only at the expense of someone else's exclusion. The strategy is simple, really—promote divisiveness and then exploit it for your own benefit.

Liberals should thank God every day for differences between people because without them, liberalism would be dead in the water. Without them, the country might have some stability. Without them, it might have a chance to survive. Without them, the problems between those who want and those who have might actually be manageable in some meaningful or productive way.

But differences have given liberals the perfect opportunity to stop any rational discussion dead in its tracks. Differences have led to polarization. Differences have led to countries within a country. Differences have led to the dreaded *xist-ism-monger-phobia*. Differences have allowed liberals to add any of these four sounds to the end of any word they choose, virtually guaranteeing that they can get away with anything they want.

Worse yet, liberals actually have the nerve to turn around and endlessly accuse conservatives of divisiveness. To them, conservatives— who believe everyone should be held to the same standards—are somehow divisive. To them, conservatives—who believe everyone should have the same rights regardless of the guises used to justify different ones for different people—are somehow divisive. To them, conservatives—who sacrifice their time, money, careers and often their lives to defend the true meaning of freedom and liberty—are somehow divisive.

But the reality is that divisiveness does not come from those who are trying to make some contribution to our society. The reality is that divisiveness does not come from those who expect others to at least try to do the same. The reality is that divisiveness comes from those who are always trying to get something out of a society far beyond what they are willing to put back in. The reality is that divisiveness comes from those who are always trying to get something for nothing.

Divisiveness in Action

Early in Hillary Clinton's autobiography, *Living History*, she makes it a point to describe her father as a "gun-loving, homophobic Republican." Despite sounding like the ramblings of an emotionally-disturbed fifteen year-old, this statement does in fact serve a very important purpose for both her and her constituency—to immediately promote and exploit divisiveness.

When Congresswoman Cynthia McKinney slammed her fist into the chest of a police officer who had asked her to show the required ID before entering the Capitol, she and her supporters immediately turned the situation into a racial issue. Why? To promote and exploit divisiveness.

During Howard Dean's short-lived campaign for President, he made it a point to tell people not to vote based on "race, guns, God and gays." Yet Dean was only planting a seed. His real goal was not to get people to forget these things; it was to make sure that they remember them. It was to promote and exploit divisiveness.

Remember the liberal claim about the 2000 Presidential election? Even though Bush won the Florida vote and all the recounts, every day liberals would insist that he stole the election—that *they* (conservatives) stole the election. Why? To promote and exploit divisiveness.

Unfortunately, just making this claim was not divisive enough for liberals, so they immediately had to include a racial element as well— to tell black people their votes were not being counted. Then, once it was clear that Gore would not be President, they made it a point to tell black people that they were now disenfranchised. Finally, realizing this strategy was too good to use just once, liberals created the whole "count every vote" farce so they could continue to promote and exploit divisiveness over and over again.

But getting back to Howard Dean—as Chairman of the DNC, he has repeatedly called Republicans every name under the sun. He has called them *brain-dead*. He has called them *evil*. He has called them *corrupt*. He has called them *racist*. He has called any effort by them to control illegal immigration the *scapegoating of Hispanics*.

Now does saying any of these things provide any sort of meaningful agenda for the Democrats? Does doing this let people know what the DNC can do for this country? Does doing this serve any constructive purpose whatsoever? In each case, the answer is no—unless you already happen to be a liberal. If you are, then it happens to serve the most constructive purpose of all—to continue to promote and exploit divisiveness.

Want more examples of Dean in action? How about the September 18, 2005 article—*Guilty of No Compassion*—he wrote about Supreme Court nominee John Roberts. In it, Dean makes all sorts of claims about Roberts including, "He has opposed various remedies for the racial injustices that have occurred in America since slavery and which persist today." Dean continued, "He has consistently joined the radical right in seeking to weaken voting rights protections, in essence attacking the rights of black and Hispanic voters."

Of course, all of this is nothing more than nonsensical statements made in order to provide a distorted view of reality. However, regardless of that, each of them does serve one truly important purpose—to incite anger in black people in order to continue to promote and exploit divisiveness. Unfortunately however, Dean is not alone among the Democrats in doing this; in fact, he's only following the lead of one of the all-time masters—Bill Clinton.

Bill Clinton practically ran his entire first campaign on a single issue—gays in the military. But why would the master manipulator possibly choose something like that when there were so many other issues the American people should focus on? The answer is simple—Clinton picked the single most divisive issue he could find (an issue that would immediately unite everyone who hated the military—homosexuals, women's groups, minority groups and scrawny liberal white men—against those who respected the military) and capitalized on it for his own benefit. In other words, Clinton focused on the issue of gays in the military because it was the perfect way for him to promote and exploit divisiveness.

Now take a look at what liberals had to say about what would have been the first step in creating what they always claim to want—a colorblind society. A society where people are judged on merit and ability. A society where everyone is given the same opportunity regardless of race, gender or sexual orientation. A society where no one cares what color you are. A society that conservatives have been trying to put in place for the past thirty years and that liberals have undermined every step of the way.

In October, 2003, the people of California voted on Proposition 54, which would have banned the State from collecting racial data in all but a few areas (such as for medical research). Of course, liberals couldn't have this because it would completely undermine their ability to provide racial preferences and would be a major impediment to their ability to promote and exploit divisiveness.

Unfortunately, because of some very poor wording on the ballot, the measure was defeated and the liberals were gloating like a bunch of kids who had just robbed a candy store. Judith Lichtman, president of the National Partnership for Women and Families said, "Defeat of Proposition 54 signifies that...those who want to deny the existence of prejudice and racism have been repudiated." Dorothea Revell, secretary of the California NAACP, announced that, "It's a great victory against racism and for diversity." House Democratic Leader Nancy Pelosi issued a statement saying, "With the overwhelming defeat of Proposition 54, Californians rightfully rejected a misguided initiative..."

Prior to the vote, California Lieutenant Governor Cruz Bustamante gave us a sample of his not-too-coherent thoughts on the situation and the Democrats in general saying "...we embrace our diversity. We don't attack immigrants. We don't attack Native Americans. We don't attack people. What we do is that we accept people and try to have everybody have an equal opportunity." The divisive message of course, is that anyone who supports Proposition 54—well, you get the idea.

So what other divisive causes do liberals support? Well, anything but English, for one. In the classroom, for voting, for driving tests, for welfare forms—sure, no problem; let's go with whatever language a person wants. Let's cater. Let's be "multi-cultural". Let's continue to encourage differences in people so they can continue feel alienated from anything outside of their own little world. The truth of course, is that multiple languages are inherently divisive, so naturally liberals have an innate need to promote and exploit them.

Clearly, it would be much easier to create a sense of unity if everyone could speak the same language. For one, they could actually communicate with each other. But even beyond that, it would save billions of dollars a year in redundancies and would be the first step in giving "under-represented minorities" the chance to contribute something useful to society so they could elevate themselves beyond the point of needing any sort of handout.

Yet liberals have no interest in doing this. Liberals want them to need these handouts. Liberals want them to be dependent. Liberals want them to feel alienated. Liberals want to keep them just where they are— as downtrodden pawns they can continue to use in order to promote and exploit divisiveness.

The Perfect Storm

On August 29, 2005, Hurricane Katrina—one of the most destructive natural disasters ever to hit the United States—swept through New Orleans. Levees broke, the city was flooded and close to a thousand people were killed throughout Louisiana, Mississippi, and Alabama. Millions of people lost power, ten's of thousands were left homeless and estimates of the cost of the damage ran as high as $200 billion.

So how did all the supposedly compassionate liberals respond to this situation? Did they try to do anything to help? Did they try to understand why it happened? Did they show any appreciation of the complexities involved in the rescue efforts? Did they show any gratitude at all to the State of Texas for taking in tens of thousands of refugees, to the National Guardsmen coming in from all over the country, to the military, to the paratroopers or to anybody but themselves? No. No. No. No.

Not surprisingly, liberals responded to the situation in the same way they respond to everything—they exploited it. They exploited it in the same way they exploit everything—by promoting divisiveness. It did take them a few days though.

The Hurricane hit on a Monday, and it was not until late Tuesday that anyone could go back into the area again. But by Wednesday the pictures were on the news and by Thursday, they were all over the papers—black people. Thousands and thousands of black people who didn't evacuate the area were now being pulled out of the water by the military, were now homeless, were now sheltered in the Louisiana Superdome and were now rioting in the streets. Liberals knew they had

8

a golden opportunity, and they were not about to let it slip away.

As expected, Al Sharpton and Jesse Jackson were immediately on the scene. "I feel that if it was in another area, with another economic strata and racial make-up, that...FEMA would have found its way in a lot sooner," Sharpton said. All of his other comments carried what was basically the same message—completely unsubstantiated claims which did nothing but promote and exploit divisiveness.

Not to be out done, Typhoid Jesse told CNN, "Today, I saw five-thousand African-Americans on the I-10 causeway—desperate, perishing, dehydrated, babies dying... It looked like Africans in the hull of a slave ship. It was so ugly and obvious." Ugly and obvious, Jesse? You mean like your efforts to promote and exploit divisiveness?

Then we had Howard Dean, who made it his mission to take a bad situation and make it worse by telling everyone that race was a factor in the deaths caused by the Hurricane. "We must ... come to terms with the ugly truth that skin color, age and economics played a deadly role in who survived and who did not," Dean said at a meeting of the National Baptist Convention. Of course, he never explained the reasoning behind his claim that skin color made a difference, but then again, that sort of explanation would hardly matter to someone whose only point was to promote and exploit divisiveness.

Unfortunately, just exploiting black people is not enough for the Democrats these days, so the next week Dean issued a press release in honor of Hispanic Heritage Month. Along with the usual divisive statements ("Hispanics are among those most affected by the devastating impact of the Republican Party's special interest agenda"), Dean continued to use the Hurricane to promote divisiveness. In the supposedly celebratory message, Dean stated that "... Tens of thousands of Hispanic families displaced by Hurricane Katrina...worked hard and played by the rules but were left behind when they needed a helping hand." The message was clear—conservatives don't care about Hispanics, and you should hate them with every fiber in your body.

Then Ted Kennedy, never at a loss for divisive comments, took his turn at exploiting the hurricane. "The powerful winds and flood waters of Katrina tore away the mask that has hidden from public view the many Americans who are left out and left behind. We cannot continue to ignore the injustice, the inequality, and the gross disparities that exist in our society."

Not surprisingly, Nancy Pelosi had been falling all over herself in making divisive statements in the days that followed the hurricane. However, two weeks later, she was still at it. Speaking at a Minority Business Summit, Pelosi said, "In the wake of Hurricane Katrina, we need to provide opportunities... but the Bush Administration is trying to undermine our efforts and put minority small businesses at a disadvantage in receiving federal contracts." Of course, she never did get to the part about how they were actually doing that.

For some other sounds of divisiveness, we need only to turn to one of the most divisive groups in the country—the Congressional Black Caucus. Rep. Diane Watson (D-CA) described those suffering because of the hurricane as "sons and daughters of slaves." Rep. Elijah Cummings (D-MD), announced, "We cannot allow it to be said that the difference between those who lived and those who died in this great storm and flood of 2005 was nothing more than poverty, age or skin color." They certainly have their agenda—to promote and exploit divisiveness.

But enough about politicians, how about divisiveness in the media? Well, to answer that question, I took a look at the September 19th issue of Time Magazine (the first issue after the hurricane hit) which featured the picture of a very distraught black woman with her hands over her face on the cover. Okay, fine; a huge percentage of the people impacted by Katrina were black, so I figured I would give Time the benefit of the doubt. Then I began to read the accompanying article. Guess what—it opened with the story of someone asking Condoleezza Rice about how President Bush "doesn't care about black people." Enough said.

Not surprisingly, the September 19th issue of Newsweek— the same magazine whose lies about Koran abuse at Guantanamo Bay triggered riots all over the world—was no better; in fact, it was considerably worse. On its cover was a picture of a black baby. Their headline: Poverty, RACE & Katrina: Lessons of a National Shame. By the way—just to be clear—it was Newsweek, not me—who capitalized RACE (in big bold letters, by the way) in their headline. Obviously, it was not enough to simply say it; they had to make sure it was the one element of the entire situation that everyone focused on. Why? There is only one possible reason—to promote and exploit divisiveness.

Of course, when things are at their worst, liberals always go in for the kill and several of them tried to exploit the divisiveness they created through Katrina into a strategy to undermine President Bush's nomination of John Roberts to the Supreme Court. In particular, Howard Dean, speaking specifically about the black residents of New Orleans said that Robert's "entire legal career seems to be about making sure that those folks don't have the same rights as everybody else does." As usual, there was no substance in anything Dean had to say, but then again, his goal was not about substance—it was simply to promote and exploit divisiveness.

Conclusions

Over the past several pages, we have seen example after example of liberal divisiveness from politicians, the media, radical feminists, minority groups and a variety of others. However, regardless what is ever said or where it comes from, by now it should be clear that a key method for liberals to use in any situation is to promote and exploit divisiveness.

But what is the point of all of this divisiveness? In other words, why do they do it? Why do people who are supposed to be adults, spend twenty-four hours a day calling people names, trying to turn everything into a racial issue, endlessly categorizing and demonizing people, and continuing to do everything they possibly can to breed the hatred they so vehemently claim to oppose? Why can't they just grow up and try to do something productive with their lives—something that does not involve attacking other people?

Well, it turns out that there are quite a few reasons for them to focus on promoting divisiveness, not the least of which is that growing up and trying to doing something productive is just too damn hard. Clearly, life is so much easier when all you have to do is promote divisiveness and then exploit it for your own benefit.

And just what are these benefits? How about special rights, privileges, opportunities and immunities endowed upon those doing the dividing? How about being allowed to take more from a society than what you put in? How about "diversity" (i.e. divisiveness) programs at companies that require them to wine, dine, attract and employ "people of color" (i.e. anybody who isn't a heterosexual white male) based on these divisions first and the abilities of the person second? How about government contracts that are required by law to be given to companies regardless of how inept they are? How about guaranteed business? Guaranteed customers? Guaranteed profits? Guaranteed success? Something for nothing. In fact, everything for nothing.

What about the benefits to the liberal politicians who are the ones ultimately keeping this divisiveness alive? What about Dean, Hillary, Pelosi, Gore, Schumer, Boxer, Kerry, Kennedy and just about everyone else with a "D" next to their name? What do they get by promoting divisiveness? The answer is they get themselves elected. The answer is they get to live high on the hog. The answer is they get to run your life. The answer is that since they offer absolutely nothing of substance to anyone, the only thing they can offer is hatred of those who do.

Make no mistake about it, each and every day there are thousands of special-interest groups—whether it be some breed of anti-male feminist, some sort of anti-business union, some sort of anti-anything-not-of-my-kind league or some group of X, Y or Z-American—continually feeding the frenzy of their members in order to keep the liberal war machine in motion. They harp on every issue. They spin every situation. They twist every word. They put up every barrier they can between people as they distort reality in every way possible in order to continually promote and exploit divisiveness.

The bottom line is that these groups will do and say whatever it takes to keep the people they cater to as angry as possible. These groups will do and say whatever it takes to keep resentment and hostility alive. These groups will do and say whatever it takes to ensure that anytime someone has the courage to step up and actually try to get people to think for themselves, that their members are ready, willing and more than able to do everything they possibly can to attack, undermine, sabotage and destroy that person.

By simply looking at the facts, the behaviors, the statements and the endless contradictions, there is no question that liberals are constantly at work to make sure the people they cater to are united together against a common enemy. An enemy who is trying to maintain some sort of order in our society. An enemy who is trying to keep the country from collapsing into a third-world nation. An enemy who is trying to tell people that hard work and education is the only real equalizer. An enemy known as conservatives.

TWO

Bad Competition

Liberalism is the single most destructive force in our society and I can prove it. I can prove it in a way that is logical, rational, simple and straightforward. I can prove it in a way that analyzes what liberalism is at its most fundamental level. I can prove it in a way that leaves no doubt as to what really goes on all around us. I can do all of these things and more by the collective analysis of a single type of behavior—competition.

Everyone competes in some way. In a prosperous society like ours, this competition is often for money, power, success or some form of recognition. In a less prosperous society however, it might just as easily be for food, shelter or whatever else a person might try to scavenge in order to keep themselves alive.

Animals do it. Insects do it. Even plants have to do it. Regardless of what anyone might say, competition is the key to survival. The only question is what form does this competition take and what can we possibly learn from it?

Since there are undoubtedly thousands of ways in which people compete, the only way to answer this question is to simplify it down to something a bit more manageable. To do this, I offer the following proposition: *There are in fact, two and only two types of competition—good and bad. Good Competition is ultimately productive to the competing elements, while Bad Competition is ultimately destructive.*

Suppose I'm involved in a competition with a friend of mine. Suppose the competition has to do with running and that I can only run for about half-a-mile before I collapse from exhaustion, yet my friend can do more like five miles. Obviously, he is better in this particular area than I am. So what can I do about it?

Maybe I can lose weight. Maybe I can start to eat better. Maybe I can get on an exercise bike to build up my stamina. Maybe I can actually take the time to do some of these things and after a couple of months I could be running five or six miles a day and ultimately end up better than he is. Whatever my final choice is though, the actions I take under this scenario actually elevate me in some way—they make me better on an absolute basis.

Now suppose I choose not do any of these things—is there still a way for me to win? Absolutely—simply find a way to lessen his ability to the point where he is no longer any better. A good way to do this might be to get him to hurt himself—to twist an ankle, sprain a knee or even to get hit by a car. I'll plan for us to go running together, then distract him at just the right time and hope for the worst. If my plan works, he won't be able to run at all and I'll win. In a sense, I've even managed to improve myself—at least on a relative basis.

From this simple example we can see that under the first scenario, I had to become better in some way; in order to win, I had to do something constructive. At the same time, we can immediately see that in the second scenario (i.e. the case of Bad Competition) the way to win was to lessen the other person's ability to compete—to do something destructive.

By recognizing that in the real world there are often thousands of constituencies competing for the same things, we can easily expand the above example by simply thinking through what it takes to become and remain competitive. Once we do, we should immediately see that in the case of Good Competition, the competing interests need to not only improve themselves on an absolute basis, but to continue to stay ahead of their competitors, they need to keep improving themselves over and over again.

Given this situation, we can now explain exactly what we mean by good and bad competition. As such, we can define Good Competition as: *Any competitive effort where a person or organization attempts to achieve success based solely on the strength of their abilities, products or services. Those engaged in Good Competition will continually strive to improve themselves, their products or their services on an absolute basis in order to gain victory over their competitors.*

On the other hand, we define Bad Competition as: *Any competitive effort where a person or organization attempts to achieve success through any means other than the strength of their abilities, products or services. Rather than working to improve these elements, those engaged in Bad Competition will typically seek to achieve success primarily through the impairment of others.*

Social and Political Implications

Now that we've established what we mean by good and Bad Competition, we can go ahead and formulate another premise and see if we can prove it over the next few pages. If we can, it should become immediately obvious exactly what the most serious threat to our society really is.

Our second premise can be stated as follows: *Virtually everything liberals and Democrats do is based on Bad Competition, while most conservative and libertarian policies are manifestations of Good Competition.*

Keeping in mind that Bad Competition is essentially the practice of bringing some people down in order to elevate others, let's take a moment to explore some everyday examples of these practices. We start with social policies.

Some of the best examples of Bad Competition imposed by the government as a result liberalism include affirmative action, quotas, preferential treatment and asymmetrical laws (e.g. those regarding so-called hate crimes). Other examples of Bad Competition would include things like empowerment, systematic bias supposedly put in place to counter some sort of societal bias, class action lawsuits, excessive punitive damage awards and the whole concept of thought crimes. Taxes, tariffs, non-profit organizations and wealth distribution in any form would also be, based on the strict definition of the term, what we would have to describe as Bad Competition.

At this point, the natural question would be why would we have to classify the above policies as Bad Competition? The answer is simple—in each case, something is taken from (or denied to) one person (i.e. they are brought down in some way) and given to another. In the case of affirmative action, a job or some other position must necessarily be denied to one person in order to be given to someone less deserving. In the case of empowerment, special rights or opportunities are given to one person while they are explicitly denied to another. In both situations (and all the ones listed above) the competing interests are not winning based on merit, innate ability or improving themselves in some way—they are winning by damaging their competitors[1].

Now that we've touched on some social policies, we should take another minute to explore some everyday behaviors which would also be indicative of Bad Competition.

Based on our definition of bringing others down, these sort

---

[1] It is irrelevant whether this damage is caused directly by the competitors or by some external force; either way, the dynamic is still the same.

of activities would include things like traitorous or seditious behavior, snide comments, hypercriticism, propaganda, sabotage, slander, anarchy, intimidation, racketeering, extortion, false accusations and labels. Some more specific behaviors would include things like throwing pies in the faces of people making speeches; screaming, interrupting or otherwise denying others their right to free speech and burning down or vandalizing campaign headquarters of an opposing political party[2].

Not surprisingly, in both social policies and with respect to personal behaviors, virtually every example of Bad Competition we have enumerated seems to be in exact agreement with the agenda and conduct of the Left. In fact, the pattern is already so strong, that we could stop right here and have already proven our point that liberalism is the most destructive force in our society. After all, if so many of the policies and behaviors associated with it are simply manifestations of Bad Competition, it should be clear that liberalism itself is nothing more than Bad Competition. And the reason Bad Competition is so dangerous is that it thrives on only one thing—the impairment of others. Over time, this continued impairment can lead to only one logical result—the complete collapse of a society.

Need more examples of Bad Competition? Just take a look at feminism. Read any feminist statements on any issue. Listen to anything they say (or, as they like to put it, "demand")—are any of their actions ever meant to elevate themselves by doing something constructive, or is the goal simply to try to get something for nothing and to bring others down? Are they ever willing to have a rational discussion on any subject (Good Competition) or do they simply attack others and call those who disagree with them all sorts of names (Bad Competition)? We know the answer.

2   Several regional Republican campaign headquarters were attacked in exactly this way during the 2004 Presidential election.

What about all the compassionate liberals who work for some sort of charity? Non-profit means non responsibility. It means no performance, no accountability and no metric for success. It means getting money without having to earn it. The reality is that corporate America is not a scam; unfortunately, non-profits often are.

"It's the economy, stupid." Remember that one? Everything liberals say must necessarily be in the form of some sort of an attack. The mantra can't just be, "It's the economy." No, that would be no fun. The mantra must necessarily bring others down. In fact, the reference to the economy is just a vehicle to deliver the real message—calling others stupid.

In talk radio, liberals are pushing a so-called "Fairness Doctrine." In essence, this means any station with a conservative talk show must also carry a liberal talk show, regardless of whether it is profitable or if a free market would necessarily support it. Clearly, the Fairness Doctrine is nothing more than Bad Competition; if someone wants a particular kind of show on the air, Good Competition dictates that they must do everything they can to make absolutely sure that it can compete on merit.

Have you ever seen a liberal campaign ad? If so, you will probably agree that they tend to serve only one purpose—to vilify the opposition, paint a swastika on someone's head, call them racists and attack them in every way possible. The sad truth is that liberal ads rarely contain anything of any substance; they simply elevate their own candidates by bringing the others down.

Moreover, keeping in mind that Bad Competition does not elevate people based on merit or through any incentive for improvement, we should note that certain political systems themselves are based exclusively on the concept of Bad Competition. The best examples of these would include Communism, Socialism, Marxism, Fascism and

Atheism[3]. Since liberalism is also a manifestation of Bad Competition, it should come as no surprise that these are the systems of government which liberals have been driving us towards for the past fifty years.

But enough about Bad Competition. Now let's take a moment to talk about something a bit more enjoyable—Good Competition. Along these lines, some of the most obvious examples of Good Competition would be things like natural selection, meritocracy, capitalism and free-markets. Other examples of Good Competition would include any sort of wealth creation, for-profit ventures (such as corporations), democracy, sports and any sort of teamwork undertaken for some constructive cause. Interestingly, not only do all of these things happen to form the basis for most conservative and libertarian policies, but they are also absolutely despised by liberals in ways no rational person could ever even begin to understand.

Transformative Processes

Why do people compete in the first place? In a prosperous society like ours, it's not for survival—from that perspective, most people have more than they could ever need. So since we clearly have no need to compete for the basics, we can make an assumption that is not completely correct, but good enough for now—that assumption is that people compete with each other because of the need to feed their own egos.

Interestingly, liberals supposedly hate people with big egos; however, the reality is that they only hate people with big egos who try to do something constructive—something based on Good Competition.

---

3   Regardless of any representation to the contrary, atheism has all the characteristics of both a religion and a political system.

In fact, it should be immediately obvious to anyone who has ever dealt with a liberal that they almost always tend to have bigger egos than anyone else around—just listen to arrogance of the way they speak.

However, putting the ego debate aside, the issue of ego and competition does raise an interesting question: Is there any way in which a society can transform ego—which we assume to be a selfish desire—into something constructive that can be used to contribute to the greater good? It turns out that by simply understanding the nature of competition, we can immediately see that not only is the answer to this question a resounding "yes," but several of these mechanisms have already been in place for thousands of years. I call these *Transformative Processes.*

Two excellent examples of Transformative Processes would be competitive sports and capitalism. As long as the participants are playing by the rules, competitive sports—whether baseball, football, running, boxing or whatever—are all perfect examples of Good Competition. The only way to be successful in these areas is for a player or team to continually improve themselves on an absolute basis.

The same is true of capitalism. Ego (among other things) can easily lead to a desire for money or power which may result in crime, frivolous lawsuits or countless other actions where someone could try to get something without ever actually earning it. However, capitalism provides a structured mechanism whereby this desire is fulfilled in a way that benefits all of society—simply provide a product or service that other people need and success will eventually follow.

Although there are certainly people who would put the effort into doing something constructive even if it did not provide any direct benefit to them, it should be fairly clear that Transformative Processes are the engine which ultimately drives society. The dynamic is simple—provide a reward for certain skills, and those skills will blossom.

Furthermore, referring back to our earlier statement regarding liberalism being a manifestation of Bad Competition, we would naturally expect that liberals would feel the need to attack anything which promotes Good Competition and logically, this would also include Transformative Processes. Of course, this is exactly what we see and both capitalism and sports are two things that liberals of one persuasion or the other constantly try to undermine every chance they get.

Conclusions

In 1975, a telephone call from New York to Los Angeles cost something like $2.00 per minute; by 2005, as a result of competition—Good Competition—it had dropped to a nickel. Unfortunately, during this same time, we have seen the standards in education decline to the point where functional illiterates can graduate high-school, college or even make it through a Masters program. Sure they may be getting ahead, but only as a result of Bad Competition. Good competition works incredibly hard to get a real education—to learn something of substance; Bad Competition on the other hand, gets what it wants by bringing the entire system down.

Lowering standards and providing special rights, privileges and preferences not based on merit, work ethic, previous achievement or future potential are all elements of Bad Competition. Those who win or get ahead in this way are usually the ones least capable of making any meaningful contribution to society, while those who lose are the ones who are most capable.

Putting aside the complete inequity of this sort of system to the victims of Bad Competition, it should be clear that the ultimate cost of these policies to our society is that the motivation for a person to elevate themselves on an absolute level will eventually cease to exist. Instead, as a result of the very lucrative rewards provided by Bad Competition, the focus will turn exclusively to getting ahead by bringing others down.

Unfortunately, because of the incredible prosperity that currently exists in the West, the large-scale effects of this increasingly pervasive dynamic are sometimes hard to see, particularly in the short term. However, in the long run, the logical result of Bad Competition is undeniable—at some point, the society will have undermined itself so thoroughly that it will no longer be able to function. However, regardless of these consequences—and solely as a direct result of liberalism—Bad Competition has continued to permeate nearly every aspect of our lives.

So what can we do about it? Well, a couple of things. The first is to be sure to recognize Bad Competition whenever we see it. The second and far more important one is to be absolutely sure the people we put into positions of power anywhere in this country promote *only* policies which encourage Good Competition. Those who do not must be kept out of office at all costs. This simple rule explains exactly why Hillary Clinton cannot ever be allowed to be President—*absolutely everything about her, whether it be her positions, her policies, her ideology, her speech patterns, her campaign strategies or anything she ever says or does is based solely on the relentless exploitation of Bad Competition.* And Bad Competition will—without a doubt—be the death of this country.

THREE

Groupdividual

Some things never change—human nature, for example. On the other hand, some things are always changing and one of the best examples of these is language. Since that happens to be the case, I feel compelled to go ahead and create a new word to describe what has undoubtedly become one of the most corrosive forces in our society—groupdividual. We start with some definitions.

With regard to people, a group can be defined as *a collection of individuals having some common characteristic*—race, for example. On the other hand, an individual is generally defined as *a single human being, apart and distinct from any larger social, ethnic or other group*. Since groupdividual is a combination of these two words, we can feel comfortable in defining it to mean, in general, the process of intentionally or unintentionally distorting the differences between groups and individuals.

More formally, we can define groupdividual as: *i) the intentional or unintentional merging of the distinctions betweens groups and individuals for the purpose of granting or denying rights, responsibilities or opportunities to certain individuals based solely on the groups they belong to; and ii) the process of invoking other members of a group when a discussion is really about a particular individual.* In simpler terms, groupdividual is any situation where someone should be talking about a specific individual and ends up involving some larger group.

Sounds interesting—but why does all this matter? Because, as I said earlier, groupdividual—which was originally nothing more than a conversational nuisance twenty or thirty years ago—has become what is now, without question, one of the most destructive forces in our society.

When it comes right down to it, groupdividual is the basis for any and all flawed social policies within the United States. Groupdividual justifies and perpetuates the systematic and ever-increasing bias against white men. Groupdividual explains why members of certain groups have—for all practical purposes—become immune to criticism and exempt from any form of personal responsibility. Worst of all, groupdividual is the exact method and means by which liberals can repeatedly get away with exercising their endless stream of bigotry, hatred, preferential treatment and outright discrimination. Like it or not, groupdividual has developed into one of the most powerful tools liberals have when it comes to undermining the very fabric of our society.

Me, Myself and Them

You know, liberals are funny. Not necessarily funny in the sense of humorous—but funny in the sense of the endless contradictions they continuously come up with and then so maliciously try to justify and defend. Yet, among all of the contradictions we hear from them, the ones I tend to find the most interesting are those having to do with the concept of individuality—a notion which they supposedly cherish above all else.

Individuality. Liberals always talk about it. Liberals always express it. Liberals always defend it—except at exactly that moment when it no longer does them any good. No, once that happens, individuality no longer matters. Once that happens, groups suddenly matter. Once that happens liberals are no longer about *me, me, me.* Once that happens, liberals suddenly become *we, we, we.* And you, you, you had better understand the fact that "we, we, we" deserve more than anyone could ever possibly imagine.

Not surprisingly, this all too common transformation back and forth between *me* and *we* is the very essence of groupdividual. After all, groupdividual is the sole basis for affirmative action. Groupdividual is the sole basis of the scam known as diversity. Groupdividual is the sole basis for any argument in support of reparations. Most disturbing of all, groupdividual is the key factor in the Left's incessant accusations of racism.

On the other hand, a true understanding of groupdividual immediately exposes and explains each and every situation where person A is systematically discriminated against or blamed for something simply for being a member of group A, while person B is systematically given special rights or privileges or revered as a victim simply for being a member of group B.

Just take a closer look at affirmative action—i.e. the institutional bias put in place by liberals based on nothing more than race or gender. Because of this policy, an individual, simply by virtue of being a member of some special "under-represented" group, may be hired for a job, promoted to a more senior position or accepted into some academic program ahead of someone else who—based purely on merit—is considerably more deserving than they are. Why? The answer is groupdividual.

Any and all arguments in support of affirmative action necessarily invoke the absolute illogic of this concept—somehow involving a larger group when the only things that matter to the decision process are the specific individuals competing for that particular slot.

Still, despite all the supposed justifications for this absolute atrocity, I have yet to hear any rational explanation for why sharing similar (and irrelevant) characteristics with other people should in any way entitle a specific individual to something they don't deserve—particularly when what they get only comes at the expense of someone else. Of course, the reason for this lack of explanation is that there is no rational reason it should ever entitle a person to anything—unless one employs the distortion of groupdividual.

Clearly, any reason to deny Person A of something which is instead given to Person B must be based solely on Person A and Person B—i.e. on *Individual* A and *Individual* B, *not* Group A and not Group B. As soon as groups are introduced into the argument, groupdividual has distorted the decision making process.

Unfortunately, the same sort of distorted logic which justifies things like affirmative action and diversity also serves to justify situations where certain people are forced to bear burdens of responsibility that others are not. One of the best examples of this is with respect to laws involving what are generally known as hate-crimes—easily one of the most ridiculous constructs of the last fifty years.

The whole concept of hate crimes is based on the false[4] and completely irrelevant premise that certain groups are systematically attacked by other groups. As a result, the proponents of hate-crime legislation tell us that the individuals within these groups must be afforded special protections in the form of extraordinary penalties for acts committed by one "type" of person against another. Worse yet, in some instances hate-crime laws are so biased that there are often consequences

---

4   See Chapter 10: Statistical Manipulations.

for situations where no crime was ever actually committed—other than the pseudo-crime of saying something "inappropriate."

But putting aside the fact that the underlying justification for these laws is in itself a distortion, the question still remains—what does this supposed group behavior possibly have to do with what happens between two individuals? How does sharing any sort of physical or psychological characteristic with other people possibly matter when it comes to the interaction of Person A and Person B? The answer is that it doesn't matter—at least not without the liberal distortion known as groupdividual.

The Perfect Excuse

So far, our discussions in this chapter have focused on providing some real-world examples of the first part of our definition of groupdividual—i.e. the merging of the distinctions betweens groups and individuals for the purpose of granting or denying rights, responsibilities or opportunities to certain individuals based solely on the groups they belong to.

However, now that we have a better understanding of that piece of the concept, we should take a minute to explore the second part of the definition—i.e. the process of invoking other members of a group when a discussion is really about a particular individual.

Of course, any rational person who has ever tried to have a discussion with a liberal about the behavior, qualifications or accountability of a woman, homosexual, black or other so-called minority will, no doubt, have experienced this aspect of groupdividual as well as the associated wrath of the liberal invoking it.

You see, the absolute illogic of groupdividual demands that in these cases, any negative statement (or even anything short of a glowing endorsement) made about a specific individual is immediately transformed into an attack on an entire group. Once that transformation is made, liberals can then immediately turn to what they do best—attack. Attack you for making a statement about a single person. Attack you for raising a legitimate question. Attack you for trying to actually make sense of something. Attack you for trying to care.

Go ahead—ask any liberal why Hillary Clinton should be President; nine out of ten times you will get some sort of irrelevant answer related to her being a woman. Now ask this same question of a feminist and ninety-nine out of a hundred times you'll get something along the lines of "you hate women!" or "what are you threatened by?" Say something critical of Barbara Boxer, Nancy Pelosi, Louisiana Governor Kathleen Blanco or any other female politician and you are guaranteed to get the same reaction. Guaranteed.

Of course, liberals don't just use groupdividual to avoid having to address questions or criticism of other people. No, liberals regularly use groupdividual to avoid having to address questions or criticism of themselves. Didn't get a job—invoke groupdividual. Couldn't win an argument—invoke groupdividual. Have nothing useful to offer society—invoke groupdividual. Did someone actually have the nerve to tell you that you had no idea whatsoever what you were talking about? Simply invoke to power of groupdividual.

You see, by consistently using the magical power of groupdividual, liberals can completely relive themselves of all responsibility for any given situation. By invoking groupdividual, they can always manage to hide behind other members of whatever group they chose to align themselves with and immediately make any argument not about them and their behavior, but about you and your supposed hatred for every member of their group including them.

Unfortunately, this second form of groupdividual is not only used by liberals when they want something to hide behind; no, this second form of groupdividual also comes in handy when members of certain groups are the ones doing the attacking. In these cases, groupdividual exists not in the form of special protections for the victims; rather, it exists in the form of justification for the crimes themselves through the invocation of groupdividual.

If a man is assaulted by a woman, liberals will almost always find a way to justify it. They'll say things like "good, now he knows what it feels like," or "men are always attacking women, so why should it matter if a man is attacked?" Other than driven by a complete lack of understanding of the American legal system, what do these and other similar statements all have in common? You guessed it—groupdividual. Not surprisingly, the same sort of reaction applies to those situations where white people are victims of discrimination. In these cases, the typical liberal response is once again, something along the lines of "good, now they know what it feels like."

Want another example of this aspect of groupdividual? How about the situation back in November, 2004 when a Hmong immigrant shot and killed five people in Minnesota? For some strange reason, the vast majority of the media coverage of this event was not focused on what actually happened; rather, the coverage was focused on stories about how the United States was responsible for the death and destruction of the Hmong people back in Laos and Vietnam. Of course, this issue (which in itself is a complete distortion by the media) had absolutely nothing to do with the shooting, but is just another example of how deeply the sickness of groupdividual has infected our society.

Conclusions

I always hear liberals bemoaning the fact that we killed the Indians (i.e. Native Americans). However, no matter how hard I try, I just don't remember doing that. Yet, for some reason I still seem to be held responsible for it. Why? Groupdividual.

Two centuries ago, some white people living in this country held some black people as slaves. Because of this, there are now a growing number of people who now support the concept of reparations and—although this may come as a surprise—I happen to be one of them. Without a doubt, I firmly believe that if person A held person B as a slave, then person A should compensate person B in some way.

Unfortunately, through the use of groupdividual, this logic has been distorted into something along the lines of "if, at one time, some members of group A held some members of group B as slaves, then all members of group A should compensate all members of group B *even though* no living members of group A has ever held slaves and no living members of group B were ever held as slaves." Of course, this notion is completely absurd, but then again it would have to be—after all, it is based on nothing more than the liberal distortion of groupdividual.

Yes, make no mistake about it, liberals love groups. Sure, they may claim to be colorblind and support equal rights for everyone, yet everything they do tells us it is just the opposite. Again, just take the case of Proposition 54 in California. In October 2003, this measure was on the ballot and—had it passed—would have amended the State Constitution to prohibit state and local governments from using race, ethnicity, color, or national origin to classify students, contractors or employees in public education, contracting, or employment operations.

Now what could be more colorblind than that? The answer,

of course, is nothing. Yet, not surprisingly, the liberals in California all screamed bloody murder about how racist the ballot measure was—in other words, how racist it was not to be racist. Ultimately, when the measure failed to pass, liberals claimed a huge victory. And just what was this victory? The victory was racism, pure and simple. And how did liberals manage to justify this racism?—By using their old friend, groupdividual.

At this point, it should be clear that all liberal social policies are completely distorted by the concept of groupdividual. It should be clear that all of their debate strategies regarding these policies rely exclusively on the crutch of groupdividual. It should be clear that all of their justifications for attacking others under the guise of justice and equal rights are nothing more than a simple manifestation of the concept of groupdividual.

Knowing this, the next time some self-righteous liberal tells you how you're to blame for a situation you had absolutely no involvement in, tell them one thing—groupdividual. The next time someone tells you about diversity, tell them one thing—groupdividual. The next time someone tells you about the justification and the fairness and the necessity of that legalized from of bigotry known as affirmative action, tell them one thing—groupdividual. The next time someone tells you about the need to help women or some other "under-represented minority" at the expense of other people, tell them one thing—groupdividual. And the next time someone tells you why they deserve to be compensated in some way because of something that happened twenty or fifty or five hundred years ago that neither you nor they had anything whatsoever to do with, just tell them one thing—groupdividual.

FOUR

Relevancy and Proportion

We all know that practically everything liberals say, whether in regard to political policy, as part of a debate or in criticism of something they happen to have a problem with is absolutely meaningless; there is just no question about it. But is there a way we can actually prove this to be the case? Fortunately, the answer is "yes," and the best way to do this is by simply analyzing the details of what it really means for something to be important.

The first step in doing this is to realize that in any meaningful discussion or analysis, there are only two things that actually matter—relevancy and proportion. Relevancy is the concept of applicability—to what extent does a particular point or statement matter to the issue being discussed? Proportion, on the other hand, is how much an issue matters in comparison to the others that need to be considered.

The second step to improving our understanding is to realize that we should be able to quantify both relevancy and proportion reasonably well as long as we apply some level of objectivity to the analysis. Clearly, in any situation, the relevancy of something may range from absolutely critical (a relevancy of 10) to one which has no applicability whatsoever (a relevancy of 0).

Similarly, proportion may also range from 0 to 10 depending on how important an issue is in comparison to the others that need to be considered. Although a particular statement may be absolutely true and completely relevant, when measured against other issues, the value of that particular point may be of little consequence.

When thinking about importance from this perspective, one thing we should immediately see is that if a statement has an extremely high relevancy along with an extremely high proportion, then the importance of that statement must also be extremely high. At the same time, we should also realize that if something has an extremely high relevancy but an extremely low proportion (e.g. the case where only one instance out of a thousand supports the statement being made), then the importance of that statement must also be extremely low.

Thinking about importance in this way not only gives us an incredibly powerful tool in terms of improving our own understanding of any given situation, but it also serves as a very simple way to immediately discredit any sort of nonsensical argument about it. In practice, the best way to do this is to simply take a moment to independently analyze the relevancy and proportion of any statement: when coming from a liberal, one or the other will usually be so low that the insignificance of what they just said will be immediately obvious—and you can now tell them exactly why.

Social and Political Implications

By analyzing the relevancy and proportion of liberal statements on just about any subject, we now have a way to see exactly why their arguments make absolutely no sense whatsoever. For example, as we have all come to realize, the liberals' favorite form of debate is to make personal attacks against their opponents, to call them every vile name they can come up with and keep repeating them over and over again. Of course, the importance of these statements in justifying their position is immediately seen to be zero since the relevancy of the personal attacks to the issue itself is clearly zero.

A closely related, but slightly more sophisticated liberal strategy is to try to discredit a person by making accusations against them—find someone who has an axe to grind, find something in their past that they can point to over and over again and so forth. Of course, in most cases, the importance of these sorts of things is also zero since their relevancy is typically zero. But let's consider the situation where the relevancy is not zero, i.e. where the dirt they have on a person is somehow related to the issue at hand.

A good example of this would be a couple of years back when Rush Limbaugh admitted to becoming addicted to pain killers after spinal surgery. Liberals, sensing an opportunity, managed to find a few clips of him from a show in 1995 saying something about how drug users should be punished and so forth. With these ten-second sound bites firmly in hand, they relentlessly painted Limbaugh as a complete hypocrite and tried using his supposed hypocrisy as a reason to negate everything he ever said on any subject whatsoever.

Now, notwithstanding the fact that the relevancy of prescription painkillers to drugs like heroin or cocaine is extremely questionable (a two or three at best), let's take a look at the proportion.

As of 2003, Limbaugh had been a political commentator for at least fifteen years. Assuming a three-hour show, five days a week, net of vacation and commercials, this amounts to roughly seven-thousand hours on the air. On a percentage basis, the collective thirty seconds of statements which liberals used to justify calling him a hypocrite amounts to roughly 0.00012% or about one-millionth of his time on the air; hardly an amount any rational person would deem worthy of consideration in terms of negating everything that anyone ever said.

On the other hand, someone like Senator Chuck Schumer (D - NY) who spends a significant portion of his time talking about the importance of the inclusiveness of minorities in government, then does everything he can to oppose the judicial nominations of people like Janice Rogers Brown and Miguel Estrada—well, you can draw your own conclusions.

The same proportional logic can be used to debunk the liberal vilification of someone who may have made some sort of inconsequential (i.e. low relevancy) mistake at some point in their lives. In these cases, liberals will do everything they can to focus the attention on these one or two meaningless statements or actions, yet completely ignore all the good things a person may have done, including those of much higher relevancy. Think about the worst thing you ever did and keep harping on it over and over again. If this was the only thing others knew about you, would they really have any way to judge the type of person you really are?

In the 2004 Presidential election, much was made of the military service records of both Bush and Kerry. But how much did they really matter? At the time of the election, Bush had been President (and therefore Commander-In-Chief of the armed forces) for nearly four years. He had never made a big deal about his National Guard service, and never used it to sell himself to the American people in terms of why he should be President. Since it was not an issue for him, its relevancy in the campaign was pretty close to zero.

On the other hand, most of John Kerry's campaign—and indeed his entire persona—were built on his military record and all the medals he was somehow awarded in just six months of service. That being the case, the relevancy of his military records was pretty close to being a ten. However, despite this, liberals smeared Bush's record every chance they could, while simultaneously attacking every effort to look into the details of Kerry's record. They made every effort to focus on sabotaging something with a relevancy (and importance) of zero, and every effort to avoid any understanding of the details of something with a relevancy (and importance) of ten.

In the first half of 2005, liberals were relentlessly attacking House majority leader Tom Delay for failing to disclose trips he made which were paid for by outside groups. Did they have a legitimate case? As it turned out, when the histories of the Senators who were attacking him were looked at a bit more closely, many of them had more unreported trips than Delay. Now comparing their trips to his is simple—the relevancy is a ten. However, if they have more, than the proportion involved is clearly greater. If relevancy is equal, and proportion is greater, then clearly their actions (or neglect, or abuse of the system) were necessarily more of an issue than what he did.

A key element of any Democratic campaign strategy is to make a big deal out of nothing—to blow irrelevant things completely out of proportion. For example, during the last few days of the 2002 Massachusetts governor's race, Hillary Clinton suddenly rushed into town to fuel a political firestorm created by Republican candidate Mitt Romney having the nerve to say that the attack on him by the Democratic candidate (a woman) was "unbecoming." This single word—completely irrelevant to whether or not he was qualified to be governor or to which of them would act in the best interests of the state—then became the Democrat's sole focus. Fortunately, they still lost.

"This country was built on immigrants," liberals always say. So?—What does that have to do with anything? At some point in history, all countries were built on immigrants. The statement is completely irrelevant to the question of immigration policy meaning that the importance of the entire liberal argument is zero. On the other hand, the argument by conservatives that immigrants bring in diseases like tuberculosis and therefore immigration needs to be controlled in some way to avoid an epidemic, has a relevancy of ten. Of course, the liberal response to this is to call them xenophobes or racists; however, both the relevancy and the importance of these attacks are also clearly zero.

Without a doubt, the media is one of the worst abusers of relevancy and proportion. At the start of the Iraqi war in April, 2003, a huge amount of CNN's war coverage was of war protesters. Every ten seconds they would cut away from the thirty-second coverage of what was actually happening and spend several minutes covering the protesters. Every minute they would be interviewing another person (from this country or another) who was against the war. Every minute was biased—every minute was out of proportion. At one point, a big deal was made that at the start of the war there were 200,000 people (the usual, highly vocal minority) protesting out in the street. In reality, out of a population of nearly three-hundred million, these people represented significantly less than 1% of those who could be out there. By the way, if any of them actually had jobs, the number would be an order of magnitude smaller.

Comedy and Comedians

Clearly, relevancy and proportion are absolutely critical to any sort of meaningful discussion or debate. But before we assume that these are the only places where these concepts matter, let's briefly explore the role of these two elements in another sort of communication—the thing we call comedy.

What exactly is comedy? According to one fairly general

definition, comedy is the use of humor in some sort of performance; according to another, it's a ludicrous, absurd or inept statement or action. However, regardless of which of these views we decide to focus on, it's fairly clear that comedy is something meant to invoke laughter.

Delving a bit more deeply into this, we can immediately see (by thinking through the sort of things which we generally find to be funny) that from one perspective, the essence of comedy is surprise, i.e. combining unrelated issues or topics in unexpected ways. From another perspective, we can also see that the essence of comedy is also exaggeration—taking something to an absurd extreme.

Now looking at what these two perspectives really mean, it should be clear that the first one is basically relevancy, while the second is nothing more than proportion. However, whereas in a logical discussion one would focus on maximizing these two factors (in order to maximize importance), in comedy the goal is to minimize these two elements in order to combine unrelated issues in the most exaggeratedly absurd way possible. In other words, the essence of comedy is to defy any sensible focus on relevancy and proportion.

The reality is that comedians spend every waking moment trying to connect unrelated items and twist reality—sometimes they manage do it in a way that is amusing, other times it's just plain stupid. Regardless, the point is that comedians are experts in presenting irrelevant information in ways that are completely out of proportion. Unfortunately, this particular expertise is often no laughing matter because it immediately explains something plenty of people must have already noticed—it explains why so many liberal commentators are comedians. *Exactly* why.

Take a look at the liberal radio network, Air America—two of their best known on-air personalities are the comedians Al Franken and Janeane Garofalo. Take a look at television; the most popular liberal talk show is *Real Time* hosted by the comedian Bill Maher. In fact, take a look at just about any comedian (e.g. Whoopi Goldberg, Robin Williams, Howard Stern, Jon Stewart or George Carlin) who spends any meaningful time talking about politics—by far, the vast majority are always liberal.

Clearly, since liberalism has no rational basis whatsoever, it would be impossible to defend or promote liberal policies with any statements that are actually important (i.e. those having high relevancy and proportion). Without this option, the only way left to do it is though arguments and statements which are necessarily unimportant; comedians (experts in irrelevancy and disproportion) are the perfect tool for this. In fact, in addition to their focus on the unimportant, comedians also have one other invaluable skill they often use to promote their political agenda—insulting those who disagree with them. Now what better qualities could there possibly be for a liberal spokesman than these?

Conclusions

Over the past several pages, we have only scratched the surface in terms of how to use the concepts of relevancy and proportion to determine whether or not something has any real meaning or importance. However, from this introductory discussion, the power of the basic methodology should already be clear.

Dissect everything liberals say; in fact, dissect everything that anyone might say. Now ask yourself what the relevancy of their point or argument actually is to the issue at hand, and then ask yourself how much it really matters; i.e. what is the proportion. If, on an objective basis, either of these elements is below a three or four (a good way to do this would be to compare them to the relevancy and proportion of any sort of related or counter argument), then no matter how high the other one may be, the statement is of limited value and limited importance.

Do this with every article you read, whether it be in a newspaper, magazine or on the Internet. Do this with everything you hear on the radio. Do it with books, with campaign ads, during a political debate or when you watch the news on television. Once you begin to consistently look at things in this way, you'll eventually find that in most cases either the relevancy or the proportion—and often both—of anything liberals say is somewhere in the range of zero to two yielding statement after statement of complete and utter garbage. After seeing this often enough, it should be safe to conclude that nearly all of their arguments, no matter how passionate or grandiose they may sound, will always have one thing in common—they are absolutely meaningless.

FIVE

Implicit Assumptions

Discuss just about any issue with a liberal and you'll almost always find that the only justification they can ever seem provide for their point of view is the conclusion itself. For some reason, they seem completely comfortable in avoiding any explanation of the logic used to develop their opinion, choosing instead to endlessly repeat this conclusion over and over again as if it actually was the argument.

Sometimes however, liberals manage to go a whole lot further, not only insisting on their conclusion, but actually using that conclusion to structure an argument which then—not surprisingly—supports the conclusion itself. This process is known as circular reasoning. However, an intermediate, though much more prevalent approach is for liberals to rely on the power of implicit assumptions.

Take a look at any liberal argument regarding so called hate speech. One of the most common ones liberals use in their continuing quest to criminalize both words and thought goes something like this—*although the First Amendment was intended to protect free speech, the Framers of the Constitution never intended for this to apply to hate*. Of course, this argument contains two implicit assumptions—the intent of the Founding Fathers and the assumption that anything a liberal might not want to hear should

45

be defined as hate. Once we realize this, the entire argument turns out to be nothing more than a house-of-cards and is only one of the countless examples of implicit assumptions liberals invoke on a daily basis.

This chapter explores numerous other examples of implicit assumptions used by liberals to shape public policy and opinion in a wide variety of areas including race-relations, affirmative action, rape-shield laws, immigration, war, diversity and others. In several cases, we also expose the key flaws contained within those arguments and—where applicable—restate them to show that without these elements, the true conclusion is often exactly the opposite of what liberals would like us to believe.

Let's Assume

Liberals love to assume. "Rodney King was beaten because of racism"—we've all heard them say something to that effect. "You know the whole thing would never have happened if he was white." Oh, I do; well tell me why. "Come-on, admit it—the cops were racist." Okay, if you say so.

I don't know about you, but I would have to think that all the other circumstances like the adrenaline of a high-speed chase, King's maniacal behavior, his refusal to stay on the ground, the drugs involved and the officer's fear for their lives having seen so many of their colleagues killed in the line of duty just maybe had a little bit to do with what happened. But don't bother trying to explain that to a liberal because they will simply circle back to their implicit assumption about racism and scream it in your face even louder than they did the first time.

Want more liberal assumptions—how about those having to do

with illegal immigration? If you happen to be opposed to it, it must be because you hate all immigrants. Of course, no consideration is ever given to the real reasons why immigration needs be controlled—you know, little things like preserving our own language and culture, reducing the risk of terrorism, ensuring that anyone who comes here contributes to the system rather than leaches off of it and to prevent the spread of certain diseases like tuberculosis, known by the CDC to have an extremely high incidence among certain groups of immigrants.

But enough about race. Now take a look at liberal environmental policies—there is certainly no shortage of implicit assumptions there. Take global warming for instance. Based on some very short term data, it seems that there has been an extremely slight (less than one degree Celsius) warming trend over the past hundred years or so. Looking at this, the logical questions would be: has this happened before and what could be the cause?

Well, in terms of this happening before, we all know about the ice age which ended around 10,000 years ago—one of dozens of ice ages over the past several million years, I might add. Now logically, if there have been all these ice-ages, there must have also been an equal number of periods of global warming. After all, something can't get cold again unless it was somehow warmed back up.

This fluctuation naturally leads to a question, that question being—what is the "right" temperature for the earth? Should it be ten degrees warmer than it is now—or ten degrees cooler?

It turns out that the answer to this question is that there is no answer. There is no "right" temperature since the earth's climate naturally goes through these sort of changes as a result of the cumulative effect of hundreds of different dynamics, most of which we have no understanding of whatsoever. But this fact has not stopped liberals from deciding that they know exactly what the right temperature is and exactly why it may be changing. They know (i.e. they *implicitly assume*)— with absolute certainty—that global warming is caused by the emission of greenhouse gases by corporations and SUVs.

What about health care? What implicit assumptions do liberals make in that area? Well, for one, there is the endlessly repeated mantra that blacks get worse health care than whites simply by virtue of being black. Although it is certainly possible that they do indeed get worse health care, I would still like to see some sort of rational study explaining why the reason is the color of their skin and not a combination of cultural, economic or other factors. Will we ever see that rational study? Of course not, it would negate the need for the implicit assumption and every tangible and intangible benefit that goes along with it.

How about second-hand smoke? Lots of assumptions in that area, particularly with respect to lung cancer. Again, are there any real studies to back up these assertions? No, because for all practical purposes they can't be backed up unless you consider making a rat live his entire life in a box filled with smoke to be a valid study.

So why can't liberals just say that they hate tobacco companies because they make incredible amounts of money and go on with their lives? The answer is simple—they can't do this because their mindset will not allow them to do this. By nature, liberals *have* to complain. They *have* to criticize. They *have* to attack. And by doing these things, they can always find another guise to extort money from some company and to hurt capitalism in any way they can. Implicit assumptions are crucial to all liberal policies because without them, they are all dead in the water.

Look at the liberal attack against religion; Christianity, in particular. Even though nowhere in the Constitution are the words *separation of church and state* ever mentioned, liberals implicitly assume that a complete and total separation must absolutely exist. In fact, the Constitution merely states "Congress shall make no law respecting an establishment of religion;" in other words it cannot just declare we will all be Catholic, Protestant Jewish, Baptist or even Muslim the way so many governments had been doing for thousands of years.

However, regardless of what the Constitution may say, this implicit assumption of the absolute separation of church and state has allowed liberals to destroy so much of our national heritage by removing crosses from state seals (California), banning displays of historical items (the Ten Commandments) and even denying people the right to say "Merry Christmas" without being harassed by them.

Then we have the implicit assumptions about corporate welfare, which liberals' want people to believe is done by Republicans to make the rich richer and benefit their friends in private industry. Of course, no one is denying there is any shortage of government waste—and plenty of blame to go around, I might add—but some of the most vocal complaints about it always seem to be focused on those programs having to do with the military.

Given this accusation, we would have to ask whether the specific programs liberals complain about are indeed put in place to benefit defense contractors, or whether they exist for some other reason. In other words, could it be possible that it might actually be in the best interest of this country to keep funding new and innovative defense systems even when there is no immediate need for them?

It turns out that an objective analysis of the situation immediately tells us that the government needs to do everything it can to preserve the ability to build bombers, fighters, missiles, tanks, submarines, ICBMs and anything else having to do with the defense of this country no matter what else may or may not be going on in the rest of the world. The reason for this is simple—if any of the pieces of the incredibly complex industrial machine are allowed to scatter to the wind, it could take years—maybe decades—to rebuild them at exactly the time we need them the most. Therefore, at least when it comes to the military, corporate welfare is not about Republicans helping the rich; corporate welfare is about keeping America secure.

So what other assumptions do liberals make about the military? For one, they assume that anyone in the military actually wants war. Of course, that assumption is nothing but nonsense and most military men will tell you that an actual war is the last thing they want—they have already seen enough of their friends killed in the line of duty.

What about the implicit assumption regarding the issue of gays in the military being the same as the segregation between blacks and whites. The implicit assumption here is that differences in behavior are equivalent to differences in race. Nothing can be further from the truth.

What about the implicit assumptions liberals make about education? Well for one, they assume that throwing money at a problem is equivalent to a real solution; unfortunately, it is not. A solution would mean fixing the educational system to focus on core competencies like reading, writing, math, logic, analytical thinking and problem solving. Throwing a few billion dollars into building nicer schools, for teaching diversity, for gay studies, for women's studies or any other form of divisiveness is not a solution; it is simply a way for liberals to feel good about themselves and exacerbate the real problem.

But what are we to make of the hatred that the Arab world has for us? Of course, liberals will implicitly assume it to be a result of this country's foreign policy—the policy of paying hundreds of billions of dollars to the Arabs each year for oil we could have just as easily taken by force.

Distorted Logic

Okay, enough about implicit assumptions for now. After all, there are certainly times when liberals actually do use some sort of reasoning process to develop their ideas and opinions. Unfortunately, the sort of reasoning they tend to use is an unusual combination of circular reasoning, implicit assumptions and fuzzy definitions all coming together into some sort of incredibly distorted logic. As a result, the actions and policies driven by this reasoning process have only one effect on our society—to create more problems for people. Just take a look at what liberals have done to the American justice system; in particular, when it comes to the concept of rape.

Because of liberals, there is now a major controversy as to what rape actually is. However, at least to me, the definition is simple and should be matched with the original meaning of the word—*to seize or take by force*. Therefore, with regard to sex, rape should generally mean something along the lines of "physically forcing sex on a woman despite her objections". However, this definition was not good for liberals because it provided a clear, logical and rational explanation of what a crime is.

As a result, in several states the definition of rape has been modified to exclude the term "by force" and include the term "without consent," resulting in a situation where sex without consent is a crime. That doesn't sound too bad, does it? No, at least not until we ask ourselves what it actually means.

Unfortunately, like everything else liberals endorse, the answer is that it means anything liberals want it to and one of the most common abuses of this new definition is with respect to alcohol. The argument goes like this: If two people who have been drinking decide to have sex, the women can later claim she was raped because it is implicitly assumed that she—as a result of her intoxication—was not able to "give consent". Although the sex was not forced in any way and no actual rape occurred—at least not in the real sense of the word—simply by changing the definition, a man's entire life could be ruined for nothing[5].

The question that needs to be asked however is — what is the crime? What's the damage? Not surprisingly, the simple (circular) answer that liberals (especially feminists) will give you is the very loud scream of "SHE WAS RAPED!"

Of course, on a logical level these responses are absolutely meaningless. A woman is assumed to an adult which means that she—and no one else—is responsible for whatever she does (even if she later regrets it). Simply put, there was no crime and there was no damage—there was only sex. So how can someone commit a crime where there was no damage? The answer is that they can't—except when liberals invoke their distorted logic in whatever it is they are desperately trying to justify.

Unfortunately, the same liberal logic also applies to the concept of rape-shield laws which dictate that the identity of the accuser in a rape case can't be revealed to the public. Yet, despite this, for some reason the person being accused is afforded no such protection. As a result, by simply being accused of a crime, a man is immediately subject to public humiliation, loss of reputation, loss of income and all sorts of other problems, while the accuser hides behind big blue dots and goes about her life without a worry in the world. The net effect of this distorted liberal logic is that the man on trial—especially if he is ultimately found

---

5   I could hear it now, the ignorant screams of "Nothing! NOTHING! You think rape is nothing!" Circular reasoning at its best.

not to be guilty—is the one who is really being raped[6].

Conclusions

Any chance you might be white and conservative—if so, you must be a racist. Why, if affirmative action were reversed and unqualified white males were to get preferential treatment over everyone else—well, liberals are absolutely sure (i.e. they implicitly assume) that you would be all for it.

Remember hurricane Katrina? The most vocal implicit assumption back then was that there would be a faster response if more of the victims were white. But what was that assumption based on? The answer is that it was based on the same thing all liberal assumptions are based on—absolutely nothing.

Do you believe English should be the official language of the United States? If so, the implicit assumption is that your opinion is driven by racism (which, by the way, is implicitly assumed to a state of mind limited only to white people).

Are you absolutely repulsed at the thought of Hillary Clinton becoming President? If you are, the implicit assumption is that this repulsion is driven by sexism (which is implicitly assumed to a state of mind limited only to men).

In the same way, liberals implicitly assume that anytime the percentage of blacks, women or other minorities in management positions within a company is not in exact agreement with that of the general population, the reason is some sort of bias. The underlying causality is never examined. Similarly, liberals implicitly assume

---

6   Rape shield laws are also a perfect example of the liberal tool of Asymmetry, the focus of our next chapter.

that anytime a minority, woman or homosexual is criticized or held accountable for something they did (e.g. Congresswoman Cynthia McKinney hitting a police officer), that the underlying reason is racism, sexism or homophobia. Conveniently, they never address the situation itself; instead they implicitly assume the reason for the criticism and attack accordingly.

Of course, when a member of a minority group does commit a high-profile crime, liberals immediately take to the air to relieve you of your ignorance. *Remember, not all Muslims are terrorists. Please be tolerant of the Hmong. Please don't hate all Asians.* Assumption after assumption. Like robots, they repeatedly say anything and everything that implicitly assumes you to be too stupid to know what to think or so racist that you might actually go out and kill a person because of a crime committed by someone of the same ethnicity.

Yes, make no mistake about it—liberals love to assume. Ironically though, there happens to be another name for the concept of implicit assumptions; it's called *prejudice*—the thing liberals claim to hate the most.

SIX

Asymmetry

A major rallying cry of the American Revolution was that of "no taxation without representation," a statement based on the simple desire of the Colonists to be granted certain basic rights that were commensurate with their responsibilities. In the more than two hundred years that have passed since that time, the country these men struggled to build has continually worked harder and harder to ensure that this fundamental principle of symmetry was applied as broadly and to as many people as possible—at least until liberalism came along.

Unfortunately for us, so many of the basic tenets of liberalism—perhaps the greatest tyranny of the 21st Century—are not only completely antithetical to this principal, but in fact revolve around the exact opposite concept—that of asymmetry—in the form of different laws, different rights, different responsibilities and different opportunities for different people.

Symmetry would dictate that a person empowered with certain rights in a given situation would also have an equal responsibility for the consequences of their actions, but liberalism increasingly denies this sort of accountability to certain kinds of people—women and minorities in particular. In the same way, symmetry would dictate that a person burdened with the responsibilities of a particular situation also have the right to exert some amount of control over that situation; however, liberalism increasingly denies this opportunity to other kinds of people—heterosexual white males in particular.

The Unlevel Playing Field

Put your personal feelings about abortion aside for a moment. The fact is that it exists and it will more than likely continue to exist in one form or another for a long time to come. That being said however, there is still another problem with abortion that has yet to be resolved—that of asymmetry.

Thanks to liberalism, despite the fact that men have no rights whatsoever when it comes to abortion, for some reason, they still have all the responsibilities. They certainly have the responsibility to support a child—even one they may not want—but for some reason, they have no power to prevent the ones they do want from being killed. At the same time however, women have the right to do whatever they want in these situations even though they have virtually no responsibility at all—at least not when it comes to the father. You see, a woman can have a child and force a man to pay for it. They can also abort a child even if for no other reason than out of spite for the would-be father.

Unfortunately, this particular asymmetry between men and women does not end with an abortion or birth; rather, it seems to continue on forever. For example, if several months later the woman is incapable of handling the stress of being a parent and ends up killing the child, liberals call it postpartum depression. If a man does it, he's called a beast. Why?—Asymmetry.

The same thing is true with regard to child custody. If a couple decides to separate, women are almost always granted custody of the children simply by default. On the other hand however, men are usually given something a bit different in the separation process—the responsibility to pay outrageous amounts of child support for the next eighteen years. So here again we have an asymmetry—women are endowed with the right to the children while men are burdened with the financial responsibility and have virtually no say in how the children are raised, where they live, where they go to school, what values they learn or anything else relevant to their development into an adult.

Of course, thanks to the Left, there are also plenty of other asymmetries between men and women that have nothing whatsoever to do with children. Take free speech for example. If a man says something a woman doesn't like—even if it isn't to her—feminists have deemed it acceptable for her slap him in the face, kick him in the groin, throw something at him or do just about anything else she wants. Does this "right to not be offended" work the other way around? For some reason, I don't think so.

The same sort of thing happens in the workplace. There, women are essentially free to say whatever they want, whenever they want, however they want and to whomever they want, but if the same woman so much as overhears a man joke about something she might not like, thanks to liberalism, the man could lose his job. And if a man happens to be offended by something? Good luck trying to get anywhere. Why? You guessed it—asymmetry.

Based on these first few examples, we should already begin to see a very disturbing pattern—that of liberalism decreeing that there shall be different laws, different rights, different responsibilities and different opportunities for different people. Thanks to this situation, it has now become perfectly acceptable for some groups of people to do certain things, but not acceptable for others. In the same way, thanks to liberalism, it has also become acceptable for some people to say whatever they want, but not acceptable for others to say anything at all.

Have a problem with Christianity? Sure go ahead and make whatever vile comments you want twenty-four hours a day no matter what anyone else might think. After all, thanks to liberalism, it's okay to call someone who believes in the concept of personal responsibility a *Jesus freak,* but not okay to refer to a mass murderer as an Islamic terrorist. Go ahead, make fun of a Texas accent—ha, ha, ha—you're suddenly a comedian. Make fun of a Chinese accent on the other hand, and you are immediately deemed to be a racist.

Any chance you remember the name Colin Ferguson? If not, let me remind you who he is. On December 7, 1993, Colin Ferguson—a black man from Jamaica—walked down the aisle of a crowded Long Island Railroad car during the middle of rush hour and started shooting white people. At the end of it all, six people were dead and nineteen others injured including some that were crippled for life.

So how did Ferguson's lawyers—along with so many other people—try to justify this massacre? Simple, it was not his fault at all—it was our fault. It was our fault for inciting him. It was our fault because Colin Ferguson was actually a victim—a victim of black rage, a concept often invoked whenever a black person attacks a white person (as opposed to the concept of a hate crime, invoked any time the situation is reversed).

So just what is black rage? What does it mean? Well, not surprisingly, like all liberal scams, black rage means anything a person wants it to. More specifically however, black rage is a liberal farce created as a way to excuse a black person for the responsibility of any crime they commit. I mean, after all, there is only so much racism and discrimination they could take before they finally snap.

Now I ask you—what would happen if a white guy were to

shoot up a train full of black people he never met because he was denied a job as a result of affirmative action? Would that be understandable? Would it be acceptable? Would liberals insist he was an innocent victim because he was overcome by white rage—or would they just focus their hatred on writing a thousand more stories about how he was just another angry white male who loved guns and hated black people? Don't bother answering—asymmetry immediately provides us with the answer.

Then we have the situation where liberals are always crying about all the opportunities supposedly denied to blacks, immigrants, women and so forth. *If only he was given the opportunity... If only she hadn't been denied the chance...* Yet when liberal policies deny a white male of something, the response is generally along the lines of "good, now he knows what it feels like." Not surprisingly, only the twisted, asymmetrical mind of a liberal could be happy when someone who never did anything to hurt anyone else would be denied an opportunity simply because of the color of their skin.

How about the asymmetry of perception? Ever hear how liberals talk about poor white people: *White trash, trailer trash, Jesus freaks, toothless, lazy, stupid, rednecks, hillbillies* and any other vile thing they can think of, right? And how do these same liberals describe poor black people?—*Oppressed, victims, downtrodden, exploited, the obvious result of slavery and institutional racism* and so forth. Same situation, but a different perception. Same situation, yet one group is ridiculed while the other is exempted from any responsibility whatsoever. Same situation, but an asymmetry of perception somehow makes them very different.

Need another example of asymmetry? Just take a look at the situation at Stuyvesant High School, the most prestigious public school in New York.

At Stuyvesant, over fifty percent of the student body is Asian. Fine with me—if they happen to be the smartest and work the hardest, then they should be the ones who are there. Unfortunately, liberal concepts of right and wrong are not nearly as objective as those of conservatives and therein lies the problem.

You see, Stuyvesant has a club—it's called the Asian Student's club. It also has club for black students. Not surprisingly, it also has another club for Hispanic students. So seeing all of these clubs which catered to students based solely on race, some of the white students—a minority at the school—decided that they too would form a club. However, for some unknown reason, the administration suddenly stepped in and stopped them. Apparently, even though every other ethnic group could have its own society—including the group which represented 51% of the student body—these particular students could not. And why were they denied the same rights as everyone else? Simple—because they were white. Asymmetry strikes again.

However, as rampant as asymmetry is our everyday life, we should also point out that liberal asymmetry is in no way limited to only domestic situations; it applies just as easily to international ones as well. Take Iraq for example. There, Muslims can feel free to blow up mosques, kill civilians, kill people on the highest and holiest of religious holidays or do just about anything else they want. On the other hand, if an American soldier does something even remotely comparable to any of these things, liberals are absolutely outraged.

But then again, liberals are always outraged. Just take a look at their reaction back in 2003 when Rush Limbaugh had the nerve to say he did not think Philadelphia Eagles quarterback Donovan McNabb (who is black) was as good as the media made him out to be.

As expected, Limbaugh's comments sparked immediate outrage from liberals and a trio of Democratic presidential candidates—Wesley Clark, Howard Dean and Al Sharpton—felt so strongly about them that they each called on ESPN to fire Limbaugh. Clark called the remarks "hateful and ignorant speech." Dean called them "absurd and offensive." The NAACP said they were "bigoted and ignorant."

Interestingly however, none of these people have ever had anything negative to say about any remarks from the likes of Harry Belafonte, Louis Farrakhan, Danny Glover, or any of the countless rap stars focused on hating white people. Why?—Asymmetry, of course (along with some pretty pathetic pandering as well).

Not surprisingly, the net result of asymmetry—just like the net result of all liberal policies—is ultimately to do nothing except create more problems for our society. You see, asymmetry allows certain people to feel an innate sense of entitlement and, more often than not, they have no qualms whatsoever about exploiting these advantages for their own benefit. As a result, other people are consistently reduced to second class citizens and the resulting resentment will eventually come back to haunt us in ways we have yet to imagine.

But even beyond this inexcusable divide, it should be clear from both the examples we've discussed as well as the experiences in our own lives, that asymmetry rewards the weak and punishes the strong. It should also be clear that asymmetry rewards irresponsibility and penalizes those who try to be responsible. As a result of these external influences, the people within our society will tend to become weaker and more irresponsible. At the same time, with so many deterrents to strength and responsibility imposed by liberalism, these qualities will continue to simply fade away. Unfortunately, both of these tendencies are exactly the opposite of what needs to happen in order for this country to prosper or even survive.

Equality of Law vs. Equality of Circumstance

Now that we've had a chance to explore some of the more obvious asymmetries that liberals have imposed on our society, I think it could be useful to take a minute to understand just how they get away with putting these mechanisms in place. In order to do that, we first need to recognize and contrast two fundamentally different kinds of equality— the equality of law and the equality of circumstance.

Although The Declaration of Independence tells us that "all men are created equal," the truth is that we are not all created equal. Some people are good looking; others are not. Some people are phenomenal athletes; others are not. Some people are incredibly bright; others are not. A few lucky people are even born into wealthy families; but unfortunately, most of us are not.

So given all of these obvious examples of inequality, why would the Founding Fathers make such an absurd statement. Why would they declare all men to be "created equal" when everything around us screams out that we are not? The answer is simple, really—because the reference to equality was never meant to be applied to circumstance or ability; the reference was meant to apply only to equality under the law.

Unfortunately, this concept—like every other one in our society—has been perverted by the Left into meaning something it was never meant to and it is through this very perversion that all the problems now arise.

Equality under the law means just that—justice is justice, the law is the law and the rules are the rules. There are no exemptions for being white, for being a woman, for being black, Indian, Chinese, a homosexual, a Christian, a Jew, a Muslim, an atheist or anything else. In the same way, equality under the law means that there are no additional protections for certain kinds of people or extra penalties for crimes committed against them—even if the left wants to invent a whole new concept in order to try to justify them.

On the other hand, equality of circumstance is a notion which is not claimed by the Declaration of Independence nor guaranteed by the Constitution and no government of the liberals, by the liberals and for the liberals has any right whatsoever to claim or impose any such thing on our society—especially at the expense of another person.

What this means is simple—liberal women, for example, have no right to go around hitting or slapping men when they have a problem with something that was said just because the men they attack might be twenty times stronger than they are. The lack of physical strength of these women is their circumstance and their problem. On the other hand, the law is the law and should in no way ever be assumed to be or used as a mechanism to compensate for her mental or physical deficiencies.

In the same way, when a liberal attorney runs into a courtroom with a poor, downtrodden client who wants to sue a multibillion dollar corporation for some supposed damage, the only issues that should ever be considered are those facts entirely revenant to the case—i.e. was any actual injury a direct result of something the company did? Any reference to how much money the company makes, how insignificant losing a few hundred million dollars may be to them or anything else having to do with comparing or contrasting the financial circumstances of the plaintiff to that of the defendant are in no way relevant. Yet this sort of thing happens all the time in our society—both in and out of the courtroom—and liberals get away with it by the simple bait and switch regarding equality of the law with equality of circumstance. However, regardless of what arguments they may make to justify this farce, we need to make sure to do one thing—not to fall for it.

Conclusions

Okay. So let's summarize. Homosexuals can criticize heterosexuals, but not the other way around. Women can criticize men, but not the other way around. Blacks can criticize whites, but not the other way around. Muslims can criticize Christians, but not the other way around.

Now Asians can always criticize whites, but they still have to be cautious about any criticism of blacks—unless the black in question happens to be a conservative. Women on the other hand can always criticize blacks—except for those blacks who criticize whites.

Fortunately, lesbians can criticize anyone they want, but no one, not even gays, blacks or other women can criticize them. Gays however, can criticize Muslims—but only if the criticism is related to homophobia and not religion. Now Christians are always allowed to criticize other Christians especially when the Christians being criticized are more Christian than the ones spewing the criticism.

Of course, fat people can criticize thin people—except fat Republicans can't criticize anyone. Short people on the other hand can always criticize tall people unless the tall person happens to be gay.

Now if you happen to be a complete wimp, you can always criticize anyone stronger than you—unless the person stronger than you is a woman in which case she every right to immediately beat the crap out of you.

Of course, this list of priorities and preferences can go on and on and we can always come up with different combinations and permutations to try to make sense of the society that liberals have created for us. Fortunately however, we no longer need to do this because now we know that all of these things—and so many others—are simply manifestations of one of the most fundamental tools that liberals use to undermine our society—the tool of asymmetry.

Unfortunately, although asymmetry has certainly come to dominate liberal thinking when it comes to race and gender, we should also make it clear that it is in no way limited to just these areas. No, liberals have managed to extend this concept as far as they possibly could and one of the worst abuses of asymmetry is now within the American legal system itself.

Apparently, it wasn't bad enough that crimes were being invented out of thin air—hate crimes, thought crimes, sexual harassment, hostile work environment, so many of the class-action lawsuits we see and so forth—but the punishment for so many of these crimes has become orders of magnitude more severe than any damage, if any, they could ever possibly cause.

Even worse, the payday for being a victim of one of these supposed crimes is often so lucrative that the alleged victim never has to work another day in their life. In short, the punishment no longer fits the crime and the incentive for creating more of these fictitious crimes (as well as for being a victim of one of these crimes) is extraordinary.

Forget the old adage about having to work your way up in the world. For a woman, being "sexually harassed" by a joke overheard at work is now the best thing that could possibly happen to her. In fact, it is actually better than winning the lottery because not only can it make her an instant millionaire, but it can also end up ruining the life of someone she may also happen to despise.

Two thrills for the price of one. Isn't asymmetry wonderful?

SEVEN

Causality, Correlation and Coincidence

One of the most effective tools the Left has used to distort reality and promote their agenda is to continually try to change the way people relate certain events to each other. In order to do this, liberals relentlessly try to obscure any meaningful understanding or discussion of why things happen, constantly try to take credit for things they had nothing to do with and continually make every effort to blame conservatives for problems they didn't cause. A typical way in which liberals achieve these goals is through the manipulation of three key elements of relational logic—causality, correlation and coincidence.

Causality is the term used to describe the relationship between two events or effects when one of them is actually responsible for the other. For example, if I light a match and drop it into a pile of leaves which then bursts into flames, it should be clear that I've caused a fire. In the same way, we all know that gravity is the reason an apple falls from a tree. In both these cases, without the first event or effect, the second simply would not happen.

A coincidence on the other hand describes a situation where

two or more events happen at the same time purely by chance; i.e. a situation where one has absolutely nothing to do with the other. If I stand in my kitchen and light a match just before a pile of leaves bursts into flames a mile away, the fact that they happened to catch on fire is nothing more than a coincidence. Whether I lit my match or not, the event on the other side of town still would have happened.

Somewhere in-between these two extremes of causality and coincidence is one other way events can be related to each other—correlation. In a nutshell, a correlation is a relationship between certain things that tend to happen or change together. However, the key thing to keep in mind is that although the events are indeed somehow tied together, neither of them necessarily causes the other.

If half the time I light a match, something in my neighborhood catches on fire, we would say there is a fairly strong correlation between my match and the fires. However, assuming there is no way my actions are actually causing the fires, there must be something else going on; the fact that they keep happening is just too much of a coincidence. Fortunately, if we take a moment to step back, we might be able to see just what that is.

The first thing we might discover is that the only time I light a match is during a blackout, so maybe something having to do with the blackouts also causes the fires. That could definitely be a possibility since a blackout could be caused lightening which could easily also cause a fire. Another explanation might be my neighbors—instead of lighting their candles and dropping their matches into the sink like I do, some people might simply throw them out the window.

Unfortunately, regardless of whatever the actual cause of the fires is, the correlation between my match and their occurrences does create a spurious relationship which could easily be exploited by someone trying to make the case that I was to blame. As a result, it is only by understanding the underlying details of this—or any other situation—and establishing a *casual* link between the specific events that we can ever hope to know what is really going on.

Stealing Credit and Placing Blame

Causality, correlation and coincidence—three words liberals don't want you to know. Spurious relationships—a concept that liberals don't want you to understand. Unfortunately for them, the cat is out of the bag. Now we can take a look at what he's up to.

Everyone knows Bill Clinton was responsible for the biggest economic boom in history—or was he? Certainly he was President during a phenomenally robust period of the American economy, no one can deny that. But to actually be responsible for something, there has to be some sort of causality. Yet, no matter how hard I try, I just can't see what it is.

The reason for this is because it is questionable whether Clinton's policies had any meaningful impact on the economy one way or another. In fact, some might argue that many of his policies (such as the ratification of NAFTA, establishing a permanent trade agreement with China and so forth) have actually hurt the economy in the long term and I would have to be one of them.

So why then was there such a phenomenal economic boom under Bill Clinton? Economists will always disagree (most of them are about as useful as a dart board anyway), but regardless of who says what, there are a number of issues that absolutely need be considered. Among these would be the normal business cycles of any economy, the end of the Cold War, the successful completion of Operation Desert Storm and the revolution in information technology during the mid-to-late nineties just to name a few.

So how much did coming out of a recession[7] have to do with the economic growth that naturally followed? I can't say for sure, but my guess is that it was probably a lot. How much did the relative stability in the Middle East (along with stable and reasonably low oil prices) thanks to the actions of George Bush Sr. have to do with a strong economy? I can't say for sure, but my guess is that it was probably a lot. How much did the end of the Cold War (a direct result of Reagan's policies) have to do with it? I can't say for sure, but my guess is that it was probably a lot.

How much did the commercialization of the Internet and all the job and wealth creation that followed have to do with the economic boom? How much did the $200 Billion or so which was pumped into the economy between 1995 and 1999 for Y2K software upgrades have to do with it? Again, I can't say for sure, but my guess is that it was probably a lot.

Of course, there is no way to accurately measure just how much each these thing had to do with the state of the economy under Bill Clinton, but it is fair to say they probably had quite a bit more of an impact than his Empowerment Zones and $500 per-child tax-credits.

I know—but Clinton turned deficits into surpluses, what about that? Well that's great, but the key question is where did he get the money? One place is obviously from the higher tax revenues which were available as a direct result of the strong economy which was a direct result of the factors we touched on a moment ago. Another place was

---

7   Which was the result of a normal economic cycle brought about by a major downturn in commercial and residential real-estate in 1989, the invasion of Kuwait by Saddam Hussein in 1990, the subsequent spike in oil prices.

from the $150 Billion reduction in military spending[8] during his first term in office, made possible in large part because of the collapse of the Soviet Union.

Causality. Causality. Causality. When it comes to the economic prosperity experienced under Bill Clinton, this simple relationship just does not seem to exist. That being the case, since Clinton's policies had very little to do with the state of the economy we must conclude that the affluence of that period was due in large part to one of the other concepts we discussed earlier—coincidence. In other words, he was lucky.

In the same way, George Bush Jr. was unlucky. The economy was already in sharp decline when he took office on January 20, 2001. The NASDAQ, which had peaked at 5048 in March of 2000, was already down to 3415 (a decline of 32%) by Election Day and ended the year at 2470 (a drop of 51%). The irrational exuberance which Alan Greenspan first pointed out in 1996 had finally run its course.

At the same time, we now know that most of the financial shenanigans at companies like Enron, Global Crossings, Tyco, MCI and others that were uncovered after Bush took office, actually happened or were set in motion during the final years of the Clinton administration. You could certainly blame Bush for them, but to do that requires ignoring one thing—causality.

Now let's switch gears. In August, 2003 a major blackout hit the Northeast and fifty-million people lost power. Instead of trying to help the situation, liberals did the only thing they ever do—attack. Hillary Clinton immediately called Larry King to say Bush was responsible because he was in favor of deregulation and because of his "coddling" of

---

8   We won't get into how much of this was necessary and how much of it was excessive; the only point is that these cuts were made possible only because of the actions of earlier administrations.

companies like Enron. Dick Gephardt cited the blackout as "... evidence that the Bush administration is inexorably tied to Persian Gulf oil and old energy..." John Kerry added, "If it weren't for this administration's obsession with giveaways to their friends in the oil business..." Blah, blah, blah.

As usual, liberals were quick to point fingers and to try to make the Republicans look bad. Unfortunately, despite all the effort they put into doing this, they forgot to do one simple thing along the way— to make any attempt to establish any sort of causality between their nonsensical statements and the blackout.

Then again, liberals have no concern for causality—just take a look at the popular mantra of, "If it weren't for France, we wouldn't exist as a nation." Amazingly, this is one of the few statements they ever make that is actually true. But the real question is—*why* did France help the United States? Was it because they cared about us, because they wanted to have us around to bail them out of all those future occupations or because they wanted us to grow into the world's only superpower so they could be sure to sabotage everything we ever tried to do? No, these things are merely coincidence. The causality—the answer to the question—is that France helped the United States gain its independence for only one reason—to undermine the British Empire, their archrival for a thousand years.

Then there is the deeper question of why do we, as Americans, actually have the freedoms and prosperity we enjoy in this county? While there are certainly a number of reasons for this, a key factor we tend not to consider often enough is the strength of our military. And why on earth, liberals may ask with disgust, is this a key factor? The answer, of course, is nothing more than a simple matter of causality—that causality being that the military creates a cocoon around the country which allows the other elements to exist and prosper.

CAUSALITY, CORRELATION AND COINCIDENCE

Without this cocoon, a meaningful industrial base could never be established and it could certainly never prosper. Without this cocoon, a first-rate technological base could never be established and it certainly could never prosper. Without this cocoon, a stable economy could never be established and it certainly could never prosper. Without this cocoon, none of us would have half the quality of life we now take completely for granted. Without this cocoon, none of us could ever prosper[9].

The whole point of a free market/capitalist society is to create a system which rewards hard work with success. Sure, some people may get away with getting a free ride through life and others may end up killing themselves trying to make something happen, but overall the system works fairly well. Furthermore, the reality of free markets is that financial success is highly correlated with hard work and in this case—even though there are other factors like luck, personal relationships and innate ability—the actual causality can be clearly established. However, liberals—in their relentless attempt to promote and exploit divisiveness—will make every effort to say this is not the case. To them, there is no correlation. To then there is no causality. To them, success is a result of only one simple, irrefutable, racist, sexist, homophobic fact of life—being a white male.

Speaking of white males, in early 2005, Harvard president Lawrence Summers was viciously attacked for trying to understand causality. He made the mistake of not hiding his head in the sand and simply accepting the politically correct dogma that men continually repress women and the only reason women (as a group) would ever fail to achieve parity with or surpass men (as a group) in every aspect of life

---

9   It can be argued that certain countries—Japan, South Korea, Taiwan and so forth—do just fine without this cocoon. However, this argument overlooks the fact that they are indeed protected by a strong military—that of the United States.

is because of this horrific circumstance which all men are guilty of.

Of course, the violent and unrelenting reaction to his raising of a very legitimate question immediately leads us to another conclusion about causality—an honest discussion on any subject will always cause liberals to throw a tirade.

Inverted Causality

Unfortunately, as if intentionally confusing causality, correlation and coincidence in the minds of the American people was not bad enough, another tactic liberals constantly use to distort reality is the use of inverted causality—blaming the cause on the effect. Going back to our first example, this would be like saying the pile of burning leaves was what set my match on fire.

Though inverted causality has certainly permeated many of the liberal lies we have to deal with every day, perhaps the best example of it would be with regard to liberalism itself—more specifically, the never-ending farce about how liberals are inclusive. About how liberals care. About how liberals want everyone to get along. And most important of all, about how liberals policies are put in place to counteract the culture of hatred that exists in American society.

Along these lines, liberals will make every effort to convince people that the policies they put in place—like affirmative action, hate-crime laws, special programs for women and minorities, and so forth—are driven by the divisiveness of our society. However, as we discussed in detail in Chapter One, one of the most effective tools liberal use to undermine that society is to promote and exploit divisiveness. In fact, it is the things they say, the policies they put into place, the race-baiting, the class-warfare, the special rights, the exemptions from responsibility and the fact that they always have to turn every single thing—no matter what it is—into a racial issue which is exactly what causes divisiveness, not the other way around.

Another example of inverted causality would be with regard to the fact that here in San Francisco, there are thousands of liberals driving around in junky old cars with all sorts of hate-America bumper stickers on them. The question is why? Now some people would claim the fact that these liberals are poor is what leads to their hate-America mentality. However, I would have to disagree.

I think it is far more likely that the *mentality* of these people is what causes them to be poor. The expectation that everything should be done for them takes away any incentive for them to do something for themselves. The expectation that everything should be given to them takes away any motivation for them to try to earn a living. The belief that everything anyone else has is the result of an unfair system takes away any reason for them to ever do anything other than complain.

Given this dynamic, we would have to question the actual cause and effect, and in doing so, we would immediately realize that for some people it goes one way and for other people it could just as easily go the other. Liberals however, will completely ignore this spectrum of possibilities and make every effort to invert the causality in every case for no reason other than to promote their own narrow agenda.

Conclusions

Over the past several pages, we have explored a number of issues from the perspectives of causality, correlation and coincidence. In some cases, understanding the form of the relationship was relatively straightforward; in other cases it took quite a bit of work. Unfortunately, for anyone genuinely interested in understanding the reality of the world around them, this work will never end.

Regardless of the underlying facts, liberals will always claim one thing causes another as long as it helps them get their way. Once this happens, the next step for them is to repeat their claim over and over again as often as possible until anyone daring to say anything different is immediately attacked under whatever guise (e.g. racism, homophobia, xenophobia, greed, etc.) is most fashionable for that particular issue.

However, despite this well-established technique of intimidation, we still have a way to unravel just about any situation to help us get a better feel for what is actually going on. That way is to simply change the supposed cause and then try to imagine—as objectively as possible—what this change would do to the supposed effect.

Would it even change at all? Why? How would it change—would it be higher or lower, better or worse? Why? Is there some sort of direct causality, or was the relationship between these issues or events purely a coincidence to begin with? Could it be that what you were led to believe was in fact not true at all and that the causality was actually inverted? Or maybe there was some other factor which influenced both of them and the supposed causality was really nothing more than an intentional misrepresentation of some sort of correlation.

Of course, the answers to these questions will always depend on the specifics of each case, but whatever the final outcome of the analysis is, always make it a point to understand the underlying dynamics of any situation. Most of all, whatever you do, do not, under any circumstances, ever take a statement simply at face value—regardless of who makes it.

Albert Einstein once said, "You cannot simultaneously prevent and prepare for war." Unfortunately, this may be the one time he was actually wrong.[10] How being prepared for something could ever be a mistake is completely beyond me. But regardless of this, the statement does sound incredibly enlightened, so of course liberals have jumped all over it as a way to attack the military, which is exactly why I see it on dozens of bumper stickers here in San Francisco every day.

But getting back to the quote, logically we would have to ask— why not? What is the causality? Why can't you be prepared for something at the same time you try to avoid it—especially when being prepared is what actually serves as the primary deterrence? The United States and Soviet Union prepared themselves for a nuclear war for almost fifty years; in doing so, they still somehow managed to prevent one. That fact alone immediately renders the statement meaningless. But even beyond that, by using this same sort of distorted logic that liberals love, the case could easily be made that you cannot simultaneously prevent and prepare for rape, so obviously the best way to prevent it would be to get rid of all the laws which make it illegal.

I wonder how many of the liberals out there would think that was actually a good idea.

---

10   Although my guess is he meant to say something along the lines of "You cannot simultaneously prevent and commit to war," which would certainly make more sense.

Revisionist History

Revisionist history is a particularly brutal form of propaganda and a perfect example of the Bad Competition continually practiced by the Left. By systematically changing historical facts, actions and motivations, groups of people with a particular political agenda can completely destroyed the foundation of a society, all of its accomplishments and everything it stands for.

Changing the nature of a conflict can make a hero look like a villain. Changing the timing of a development can make a genius look like a plagiarist. Placing events out of context can make absolutely anything look like whatever the Left wants it to. At the same time, those who practice revisionist history can effortlessly elevate themselves and their agendas by taking credit for every meaningful accomplishment of a society while blaming those who oppose them for every problem.

Not that revisionist history is anything new; after all, it was commonly practiced in ancient cultures by monarchs who wished to disgrace or belittle the accomplishments of their predecessors as a way to elevate their own greatness. In these cases, statues and other tributes to the earlier leaders were systematically destroyed. Books and records of their reign were burned. People were forbidden to mention their names.

HOW THE LEFT WAS WON

Over time, they were completely forgotten and their accomplishments subsumed by those who had erased them from history. It was only by tediously piecing together the modest fragments of evidence that survived, that historians have come to even know of their existence.

Unfortunately, modern-day revisionists are no different than their ancient counterparts, continually making every effort to belittle the accomplishments of those they wish to undermine, subjugate, humiliate or destroy. Usually operating under the guise of some form of social justice—typically things like inclusion, diversity, peace, justice or human rights—they are in reality motivated by their own hatred, fear and insecurity and will go to any length in order to make others look bad. Unable to deal with legitimate facts or historical events in a logical, rational or mature manner, they instead work to change the underlying nature of the debate by rewriting every situation to fit their own petty needs.

Unfortunately—as if all of this were not bad enough—not only are the facts being changed to suit the agenda of the people entrusted with preserving the past, but the laws of the society are quickly degenerating to the point where any reference to legitimate facts, or any debate not in line with the narrow agenda of the Left, are subject to immediate consequence either through intimidation, slander or—if liberals like Ted Kennedy and Hillary Clinton get their way—imprisonment for so-called hate speech.

Slowly, all around us, the past is being erased, the statues and monuments are being destroyed, the books are being burnt and the people forbidden to speak of things the way they really were.

Inventing Yesterday

Every day liberals tell us that Islam is a religion of peace. Unfortunately, based on what we see going on all over the world—beheadings in the name of Allah broadcast over the Internet, planes flying into buildings, suicide bombers intentionally killing civilians, Iranian Mullahs calling for the annihilation of Israel, thousands of anarchists rioting for weeks on end over a cartoon, trains blown up in Spain, subway stations bombed in London, ten-thousand cars torched in France and an assortment of other Muslim atrocities in Indonesia, Chechnya and other places—there just might be a chance that this mantra of the Left may not be as cut and dry as some people would like to believe.

Yet, regardless of this, liberals can still find plenty of ways to excuse the inexcusable and one of these is through the use of revisionist history. You see, liberals will tell you that Islam is no more violent that Christianity and point to the Crusades of the 11th, 12th, and 13th centuries as proof. Of course, not withstanding the fact that nothing from a thousand years ago could ever justify the behaviors of today, liberals will still constantly try to position the Muslims of the past—just as they do the Muslims of the present—as nothing more than victims of Christian aggression.

Somehow liberals have people convinced that the Crusades were actually unprovoked Western invasions into Muslim homelands when in fact, they were almost all direct responses to Muslim invasions into Europe or into Jerusalem and its surrounding areas. Yet, by rewriting history, liberals no longer have to face the realities of the 21st Century or come to any logical conclusions about them. Instead, they can immediately justify their camaraderie with those intent on destroying America based on the events of a thousand years ago—regardless of whether they happened or not. Besides, attacking Christianity has always been a major focus of liberalism, so why not try to reinforce every misconception about it every chance they get?

Speaking of which—have you heard about the liberal plan to rewrite the Bible? That's right; it was not enough to merely attack Christianity, now they have to change it too. After all, there was just way too much sexism and inequality in the writings of those dead white males—you know, guys like Matthew, Mark, Luke and John—and Christianity was not nearly as inclusive as it should be. The solution for liberals of course, is not to try to understand the message; the solution is for liberals to change the message to fit their own petty needs by making the bible gender-neutral.

Gender-neutral—a simple way for liberals to change what was into what they want it to be. A simple way to revise history in order to belittle the accomplishments of those they so desperately need to undermine, subjugate, humiliate or destroy. People like those racist, sexist and no doubt homophobic white men formally known as the Founding Fathers. Want to revise history in that department? Simply delete that term from the language and replace it with a more gender-neutral one—Framers.

By the way, speaking of the Founding Fathers—and despite what liberals may say—these men never did put anything into the Constitution about the separation of church and state. But regardless of this fact, whenever any important religious issue needs to be addressed—like whether a Christmas tree should be allowed on public property—liberals always repeat this concept like a mantra. Why? Revisionist history. Always easier to claim something that never was than to try to argue a point rationally. Take the situation with Joe McCarthy for example.

Liberals love to portray McCarthy as a power hungry Republican intent on destroying our civil liberties. Yet, the irony is that Senator

McCarthy was not trying to destroy America—he was ahead of his time in trying to save it by ensuring the seditious, traitorous and anti-capitalist behavior which we see more and more of each day never had a chance to take root in this country. Unfortunately, it already had—and it destroyed both him and his reputation as a result.

Another high-profile Republican target of liberal revisionists is Abraham Lincoln—one of the greatest men in American history and a personal hero of mine. Some liberals claim that Lincoln was gay— why after all, he was so soft spoken and caring that he just had to be. Other liberals will scream out that despite freeing the slaves and paying the ultimate price for doing so, that Lincoln was a racist. Still others absolutely insist that Lincoln was so "open-minded" that he would have supported all sorts of liberal causes like gay marriage, affirmative-action and special rights for women. Fortunately, since all of these claims completely contradict each other, Lincoln's true legacy has yet to be tarnished.

But liberals never stop trying to rewrite the past, and some more recent examples of their revisions would include the lie that Bill Clinton and the Democrats were responsible for the economic boom during the nineteen-nineties while George W. Bush and the Republicans were responsible for the collapse of the dot-com bubble and the subsequent recession. Of course, these fables have about as much basis in reality as the endlessly repeated story in which the Republicans stole the 2000 Presidential election.

Still, these fairly recent examples of liberals rewriting every situation for their own benefit does help provide us with another valuable insight—that insight being that revisionist history is in no way limited only to a misrepresentation of the past, but is also happening right before our eyes in terms of the events going on around us each and every day.

But how can this be—how can what is happening right now be interpreted as anything else other than what it actually is? The answer is simple—the way the media reports the news immediately creates a permanent record that can be used not only to alter our collective perception of the world around us, but can eventually be used for the same purposes as the modern-day revisions of historical events from centuries ago.

One example of this would be with respect to racism and the whole concept of "hate-crimes." Take the situation back in July, 2005, where a black man fatally stabbed a 56 year-old mother of two at a mall in White Plains, New York because he wanted "to kill a white person." "All I knew was she had blond hair and blue eyes, and she had to die... I didn't care, as long as she was white," he said.

Unfortunately, most people have never heard of this story because it was barely covered by the liberal media. Worse yet, the few who did hear of it are more than likely not to remember the name Phillip Grant because his crime did not become the center of a media circus. On the other hand, more than twenty years later, just about anyone over thirty would remember the name Bernhard Goetz—the white man who shot (but did not kill) the four black teenagers who tried to rob him on the New York City subway.

The Myth of American Imperialism

Perhaps no concept has been used more often to justify the hatred of the United States by its enemies—both foreign and domestic—than the myth of American imperialism.

Listening to liberals, you would think that this country is nothing more than an evil empire that has spent the past hundred years enslaving entire populations, undermining peace and harmony, stealing oil from poor Arab nations and working around the clock to take over the world. None of this is true, of course—but then again, the truth has never gotten in the way of the liberal agenda, has it?

The fact is that the United States is the only country in history that has not tried to establish an empire when it had the chance to do so. Unfortunately, the same cannot be said for some of our harshest critics including Germany, France and Russia, nor could it be said for more benign countries like Great Britain, Japan, Spain or even Holland.

Furthermore, in 1945 when the US—which had just liberated all of Europe from the Nazis and freed the entire Pacific Rim from the Japanese—had sole possession of the atomic bomb, not only did it not try to establish an empire of its own, but it actively discouraged European countries from trying to re-establish their existing empires which had already begun to unravel as a result of the war.

Okay, so America did not take over the world when it has the chance—but look at all the wars we have caused. After all, liberal historians tell us that both the Korean and Vietnam wars were caused by American Imperialism, right? Wrong.

The reason for the US involvement in both these situations was not imperialism as the Left would have us believe, but to stop the advancement of Communism—a political ideology based on Bad Competition,[11] openly dedicated to the eradication of capitalism and completely antithetical to the concepts of liberty and freedom that liberals claim to hold so dear.

Fortunately, at least when it came to the situation in Korea, the U.S. was successful in saving the South from annexation by the North. As a result, South Korea has had the chance to prosper, to become a

---

11   See Chapter 2 for more information on this concept.

technological and economic superpower and to provide an incredibly high standard of living for its people. The North on the other hand is nothing more than a rouge police state mired in poverty with no export at all other than weapons systems to other countries also hostile to the U.S.

Unfortunately, the situation in Vietnam—a former colony of the French, by the way—was a different story. There, liberals successfully undermined the war effort and forced the U.S. to leave South Asia with its tail between its legs. As a result, all of Vietnam soon fell under communist control as did neighboring Laos, where the communist leader Pol Pot subsequently killed nearly two million of his own people.

Okay, so American imperialism was not behind the wars in Asia—but American imperialism is definitely the driving force behind the invasions of Afghanistan and Iraq. Well, not quite; I think the need to protect ourselves against terrorism and from governments openly hostile to us while simultaneously freeing millions of people from the tyranny imposed by the likes of Saddam Hussein and the Taliban just might have had a little bit to do with it.

But American imperialism is absolutely, positively the reason the Arabs hate us. No one can deny that. After all, plenty of so-called liberal intellectuals have often said how the US deserved what happened on 9/11 and that we had it coming to us after all we did to those people.

After all we did? You mean like trying to pull them out of the dark ages? Like transforming those barren wastelands from some of the poorest countries on Earth to some of the wealthiest? By paying hundreds of billions of dollars a year for oil that we could have just as easily taken by force? Please, don't get me started. By the way, after watching the behavior of our friends in the Arab world over the past few years, God only knows what they would have done to us if the situation were reversed—i.e. if they had nuclear weapons and we didn't.

Oh boy, I could hear it now. "That's it! That's a perfect of example of American imperialism," liberals would say. "We're the only country in the world that has used nuclear weapons!"

So? So what? Contrary to liberal revisions of history, Japan—which had launched a world war that ended up killing tens of millions of people—had no intention whatsoever of surrendering before the US dropped the atomic bombs on Hiroshima and Nagasaki. The only way to prevent the loss of another hundred-thousand American lives (at least) that an invasion to end the war would have cost us was to be sure that the Japanese immediately agreed to an unconditional surrender. End of story. One of the harsh realities of life is that bringing an end to war often requires extreme measures, as does ending terrorism and insurgency. Yet another lesson from history that liberals have conveniently forgotten.

Well, at least you can always go to a museum to get the truth, right? Don't count it. These days, museums are no longer place to go to educate yourself or learn about the past. These days, museums have become nothing more than tools of indoctrination. Just take a look at the exhibit that the National Air and Space Museum had planned to mark the 50th anniversary of the end of WWII. Among other things, it would have provided some very valuable and often overlooked insights into the war including "For most Americans, it was a war of vengeance. For most Japanese, it was a war to defend their unique culture against Western imperialism," and "Some have argued that the United States would never have dropped the bomb on the Germans, because Americans were more reluctant to bomb White people than Asians."

Now go tell that to your children. Then again, never mind—the liberals running your school system already have.

Conclusions

So what can we do about the ever-increasing tendency toward revisionist history which liberals are so gleefully using to help undermine the fabric of our society? The answer, unfortunately, is not very much.

Because there is often no easy way to get back to the truth once a distorted version of the past begins to take hold, revisionist history is an extremely effective tool for liberals. In particular, once someone is raised in an environment where they are led to believe a certain set of circumstances and events, it becomes almost impossible to convince them that what they know is wrong[12]. This, of course, explains why so much effort is being put into rewriting the history books used in our elementary and middle schools.

So given this psychological limitation, as far as I can tell, there are only two ways to deal with revisionist history—either make every effort to prevent it from permeating the educational system and the public discourse in the first place, or teach people to know how to recognize it when they see it. Unfortunately, neither of these options seems very practical. Preventing the creation and dissemination of endless amounts of revisionist history would involve an incredibly coordinated effort requiring a massive amount of time and resources and is quite honestly, a battle that cannot be won.

Liberals dominate the media, so trying to put out enough books, movies or television shows to tell it like it is simply is not a viable option. Liberals dominate academia, so trying to teach history—whether to ten year-old kids or thirty year-old graduate students—with an honest and

---

12   This is particularly true when what they "know" either reinforces or justifies their reasoning when it comes to the sort of things they would like to believe anyway (such as America and white men being the root of all evil).

balanced perspective is just not a viable option. Liberals dominate the social sciences so museums, archeology, anthropology and culture all reflect the perspectives they want others to share. Trying to change all of that is just not a viable option.

Unfortunately, teaching people how to recognize revisionist history is not a very viable option either. Sure, some people may be able to do it—mostly those who are truly experts in a particular field—but in most cases, people will just take whatever they see or hear at face value. The only time revisionist history may be immediately obvious them is when they themselves have seen the historical account of a particular situation change over time (as was the case with the Smithsonian exhibit we just discussed which blamed WWII on American Imperialism).

Ultimately, it would seem that when it comes to revisionist history, there really isn't very much we can do about. Even worse is the fact that this increasingly prevalent trend of not facing the realities of history—especially without regard to the concepts of Relevancy and Proportion discussed in Chapter 4—necessarily leaves us in the position of never truly understanding the dynamics of human, social and cultural behavior. It leaves us in a position of not having learned from five-thousand years of recorded history and experience. It leaves us in the position of making the same mistakes over and over again because we have deluded ourselves into thinking that A does not lead to B and X does not lead to Y. It puts us in the position of repeating the mistakes of history simply by not being aware of them in the first place.

Clearly, liberals are trying to rewrite history. Clearly, liberals are tying to distort facts, actions and motivations to fit their own narrow agenda. Clearly, liberals are working day and night to try to take credit for every accomplishment and blame those who dare to oppose them for every problem. So given this concerted effort by liberals to continually undermine our society through the use of revisionist history, I thought it would only be appropriate to conclude this chapter with a little revisionism of my own—a revision of a Beatles song written by Paul McCartney over forty years ago. A revision, appropriately, of *Yesterday*.

Yesterday

Yesterday, all we've done is somehow swept away
Now for all our sins we'll have to pay
Oh, don't believe in yesterday.

Suddenly, we're not half the race[13] we used to be,
There's so much blame that's hanging over me.
Oh, yesterday changed suddenly.

Why facts have to go, I don't know Dems wouldn't say.
But when liberals whine, they're such swine so they always get their way.

Yesterday, changing it is such an easy game to play.
Everything you've done just fades away.
Oh, don't believe in yesterday.
Mm mm mm mm mm.

---

13   Americans.

NINE

The Perpetual Motion Machine

When I was a child back in the early seventies, I thought I had developed what was sure to be the most absolutely brilliant solution to the energy crisis the country was facing at that time. It could immediately rid us of our dependence on foreign oil. It could immediately eliminate all the frantic concerns everyone seemed to have over nuclear energy. It could immediately reduce our heating and electric bills from hundreds of dollars a month down to a few pennies. Unfortunately, there was only one problem with it—it would never work.

You see, the system my creative, though not-necessarily practical seven-year old mind had designed was one where an electric motor would be used to run a generator to create electricity. A portion of this electricity would then be used to drive the motor to continue turning the generator, while the rest could be added to the power grid and used for everything else. Simply build a few thousand of these and we would have all the electricity the country would ever need.

Now despite sounding like a simple and obvious solution to an incredibly complicated problem, my device turned out to be an absolutely ridiculous idea. It was ridiculous because I had looked at the problem only superficially and had failed consider one of the most basic laws of physics—the conservation of energy—which dictates that even under the best case scenario, the generator would barely be able to put out enough electricity just to keep the motor running. By overlooking this simple fact, I had made the classic mistake of trying to get something for nothing. I had fallen into the trap of trying to build what was known as a perpetual motion machine.

Unfortunately, liberals fall into this trap every day of their lives. However, with the right framework and a little bit of logic, we can easily show that all of their policies—economic, military, social, foreign or domestic—though always sounding like simple and obvious solutions to complex problems, are ultimately based on nothing more than a superficial understanding of the situation at hand.

In the same way, we can show that one of the most common flaws among all of them is the illusion of actually getting something for nothing. Furthermore, we will also see that in the vast majority of cases, the ultimate result of liberal policies is to actually perpetuate the very problems they so vehemently purport to solve.

Something for Nothing

Since the Federal government has the power print as much currency as it wants, a perfect way to solve the so many of the country's problems would be for it to simply print up a whole lot of money and just go ahead and give everyone a couple of million dollars. By doing this one simple thing, each and every person could instantly be a millionaire.

So why doesn't the government do this? Is it because Bush is too stupid to have thought of it? Is it because the government is racist? Is it because of a Republican conspiracy to keep everyone poor and oppressed? Or could it possibly be for some other reason? Let's take a look.

First of all, if everybody suddenly had a couple of million dollars, there would not be much incentive for most people to go to work. That could certainly be a problem because if nobody worked, the entire society would collapse. However, let's assume that there might still be some people who do have an interest in doing their jobs—but only if they were to get a significant increase in pay. After all, why would someone kill themselves for five or six hundred dollars a week when they already have a couple of million in the bank? The answer is they wouldn't and their salary would have to go up accordingly—just like the price of everything else if there was so much money floating around.

But when prices go up like this (inflation), the value of money goes down in proportion. So at the end of the day, even though we all might have a lot more cash then when we started, nobody is any better off as a result. The laws of economics are no different than the laws of physics—no matter how hard you try, you just can't get something for nothing. Yet for some reason, liberals continually try to defy this simple law. Take the endless mantra of wanting to dramatically increase the minimum wage for instance.

Superficially, increasing the minimum wage sounds like a great idea. After all, nobody should have to work for five or six dollars an hour, right? Although I happen to agree with that premise in general, the situation isn't quite that simple.

Every company has a limited amount of capital to work with and has to continually find ways to use it to cover their expenses ranging from rent, raw materials, advertising, insurance, lawyers, accountants and just about anything else you could think of. Add to this, the fact the owners need to make money (whether they be sole proprietors or investors who only put money into something if they can see some sort of reasonable return on it) and we find that in most cases, there really is not that much to go around.

Now given this constraint, if the amount of money a company has to pay each of its employees goes up, the amount available for other things goes down—not a good situation to be in. So either these added costs need to be passed on to consumers (which may or may not be practical), or the number of employees needs to go down to keep the total expenses in the range of where it originally was. Sure the remaining workers may end up making a little more money, but since there are fewer of them around, they'll probably end up working harder to get it. At the end of the day there really is no gain at all—especially when the people who have lost their jobs are factored into the equation. Unfortunately, just as governments cannot increase the standard of living by simply printing more money, neither can a business.

However, looking beyond this basic economic argument, we can also see a variety of other problems associated with increasing the minimum wage. For one, doing so provides an incentive for companies to hire people off the books to avoid paying them the minimum wage. But as long as companies are paying people under the table, they may as well get the cheapest ones they can find—illegal aliens. So now we have a situation where a liberal policy is not only driving up unemployment, but it is also reducing the number of jobs available to Americans and providing more incentive for illegal immigration. Liberals can stomp their feet all they want, but regardless of whatever they may say, there is simply no free ride.

What about taxes? Liberals love to tax. Income tax. Capital gains tax. Tobacco tax. Payroll tax. Luxury tax. But taxes are nothing more than a deterrent to working, a deterrent to investing and a deterrent to spending money, so ultimately they do nothing but slow economic activity and reduce the tax base. This then requires higher (or broader) taxation to generate the same amount of revenue, but then this further depresses economic activity. It may be a vicious cycle, but then again no matter what you do, you just can't get something for nothing.

How about corporations? Liberals hate corporations. They hate profits. They hate management, CEOs, boards of directors and anything having to do with capitalism. But where do things come from? Where did the computer I'm working on come from? A capitalist. Where did the car you drive come from? A capitalist. Where did the organic banana your friendly neighborhood liberal ate this morning come from? A capitalist.

So let me get this straight—liberals want to destroy capitalism so there are no cars, there is no oil, there is no food, there is no phone system, there is no Internet, there are no books and there is no innovation. Liberals want to destroy capitalism so there are none of these things, yet they expect them to all somehow still be around. Talk about trying to get something for nothing.

Then we have the case of affirmative action. Doesn't this supposedly benign policy of race and gender based discrimination actually create opportunities for people? Of course it does, but the question is—where do these opportunities come from? Not surprisingly, opportunities created by affirmative action come only at someone else's expense.

So what other ways do liberal try to get something for nothing? How about the whole concept of pacifism, for one? Of course, I'm not talking about rational pacifism; what I am talking about however is *radical* pacifism—liberal pacifism. The "do nothing under any circumstances" sort of pacifism. But doing nothing and expecting to get the result you want is the definition of a perpetual motion machine. The only difference between pacifism and other liberal policies is that instead of doing something and trying to get more out of it than what was put in, pacifism seeks to do *nothing* and get more out than what is put in.

How about the liberal farce of self-esteem? These days, people don't need to worry about actually being good at something; instead, liberals just want them to be told they are good. Liberals would never want a kid to be left-back in school—after all, that might hurt his self-esteem. A child could never not be picked for something she is not able do—after all, that might hurt her self-esteem.

But isn't that the whole point of self esteem—to give people a reason not to fail? To make them understand that they might not be good at something and then take the initiative to make themselves better? Isn't that the exact dynamic that motivates people to do more, to learn more, to think more and to be more confident in their abilities because they have actually developed some sort of ability to be confident in?

Not surprisingly, liberal self-esteem does none of these things. Liberal self-esteem is a charade; an illusion. Liberal self-esteem does nothing but give people an excuse to not have to develop any skills or abilities. Liberal self-esteem is just one more example of liberals trying to get something for nothing.

Nothing for Something

Other than always trying to get something for nothing, another characteristic of all-too-many liberal policies is that no matter how much time, money or effort is ever put into them, you can almost always count on getting nothing back in return. Even beyond that however, liberal policies—in addition to providing the worst possible return on investment—almost always end up perpetuating the very problem they claim to solve. Just take a look at welfare.

Welfare was meant to be a short term fix, a safety net put in place to help people get back on their feet. Unfortunately, because of liberalism, welfare has evolved from an uncomfortable situation which people would normally try to avoid, to a multi-generational lifestyle that plenty of people are more than happy to sign up for.

Worse yet, welfare creates dependency, removes so much of the incentive for people to get any sort job, provides people with the time and resources to get themselves into more trouble, promotes having more unwanted children and serves to perpetuate problems not only for those people already on welfare, but for generations to come.

So is there any way to make welfare less of a chronic problem? Of course there is. How about the idea of mandatory Norplant[14] for welfare mothers to ensure they don't have more kids? Liberals say that would be racist. How about mandatory jobs like street cleaning or some other sort of manual labor that would require welfare recipients to contribute something to society in exchange for what they get? Liberals say that would be a violation of civil rights. How about instead of mailing the checks out, we actually make people take the initiative to go down to the welfare office to pick them up themselves? Liberals say that would be degrading.

The net result of decades of liberal policies and obstruction is to make welfare easier to get, to remove any stigma associated with it, to reward people on welfare for exactly the wrong behaviors and to remove any incentive whatsoever for getting off of it. So now, instead of people avoiding welfare, they flock to it. Instead of women on welfare having fewer children, they have more—and increase their benefits as a result. Instead of solving the problem, liberals have only made it worse.

What about illegal aliens? Well, liberals certainly want nothing to do with protecting the borders. Liberals want nothing to do with deportation. Liberals want nothing to do with anything that would even

---

14   A long acting (up to 5 years) contraceptive surgically implanted into a woman's arm.

come close to solving what has become a major social and financial crisis within this country.

Instead, liberals want to welcome illegal aliens with open arms and open wallets (as long as it isn't theirs). Liberals want to provide illegal aliens with all sorts of social services. Liberals want to grant driver's licenses to illegal aliens. Heck, some liberals even want to give illegal aliens the right to vote.

So tell me again—how do liberal policies help solve the problem of illegal immigration? The answer is they don't—they only perpetuate it.

What about improving race relations? Liberals are always telling everyone how they want to do that. Multiculturalism, right? Wrong.

The United States is supposed to be a melting pot; unfortunately, because of liberalism, way too many of the people who come here are not melting—instead, their focus is to retain their own culture. Now that in itself is not necessarily a bad thing; however, the problems arise when these groups expect the rest of the country to cater to them in their own language, in their own laws and in their own way. The truth is that multiculturalism leads to isolation. Multiculturalism leads to countries within a country. Multiculturalism leads to perpetuating differences between people. Ultimately, multiculturalism will lead this nation into complete chaos.

The same is true of the other liberal euphemism for anything anti-male or anti-white—diversity. The whole diversity scam has done nothing for society except exclude certain people for the benefit of others, create an entitlement mentality among women and minorities and fuel resentment among whites and men. Not only does diversity exacerbate race relationships, but by moving the focus away from quality and meritocracy, it serves to lower the standards for the entire society at the very same time.

Then consider the case of how liberals want the military to fight a war. By being sensitive, of course. By being nice. By being politically correct. By letting situations drag on year after year, by attacking and undermining the military every chance they get and by never allowing them to do the job right the first time. Liberal policies hurt the military, they hurt morale, they costs lives and resources, and they destroy the will of the American people to take any sort of conflict to its necessary conclusion.

What about liberals and education? Surely, all the money they demand for education must have some sort of positive impact on our children. Unfortunately, that is just not the case. You see, the reason liberals always want more money is not to teach science, not to teach math, not to teach logic, responsibility or analytical thinking. Liberals want more money in order to build nicer schools, to add more layers of bureaucracy into the educational system and to have more resources to indoctrinate children with anti-Americanism, gay-studies, African-American studies, women's studies, activism and any other sort of divisive nonsense they cram into a child's mind. The reality is that liberals don't want more money for education—they want it for reeducation.

How about the liberal plan to deal with the country's drug problem? Any chance they might want to make drugs like heroin, cocaine, marijuana or ecstasy harder to get? Of course not. Maybe they want to increase penalties for drug abusers or pushers? Not last time I heard. Well they must want to encourage people—especially children—to stay away from drugs and not to experiment in the first place? No; liberals have no interest in doing any of these things.

Instead, the liberal solution is to legalize drugs—or at least give out free needles to people so they can shoot up without worrying about getting some sort of disease in the process. That's right; liberals want to prevent drug abuse by making drugs more accessible and by taking away whatever remaining fear someone might have of using them. Like everything else they involve themselves in, the liberal solution to the drug problem only makes it worse.

But what about the homeless situation—how do liberals deal with that? All we need to do to answer that question is to take a look at one of the most liberal cities in America—San Francisco. Not surprisingly, San Francisco has the highest per capita prevalence of chronic homelessness of any city in the United States. The reason of course is that the city is run by liberals and all their policies are tailored towards making it as painless as possible to be homeless. However, no thought is ever given to actually solving the problem itself.

Want more? What about the study published in a Canadian Medical Journal which claims that free drinks actually improve the lives of alcoholics? According to the article *Study Toasts Free Drinks for Homeless Alcoholics* that ran on Jan 05, 2006 on Breitbart.com:

> Seventeen chronic alcoholics who drank upwards of 46 glasses a day over the past 35 years... were offered a glass of wine or sherry each hour... over five to twenty-four months... "Once the craziness of their alcoholism is under control ...they're interesting people and all that destructive behavior is behind them," an author of the study said.

Is it any surprise that this study comes from Canada, a major North American repository of liberalism? Not to me. After all, liberals of all persuasions seem to have an innate need to find ways of perpetuating problems and giving alcoholics free booze twenty-four hours a day is probably a good example of this.

But forget about drugs and alcohol—how do liberals want to

deal with obesity? Do they want to teach disciple or self-control? No; these concepts have no meaning to liberals. Do they want fat people on airplanes to pay for the two seats they may take up? Of course not—that would be discriminatory. Do they want more physical education at public schools? Not as long as the kids have to do something athletic that might hurt their self-esteem.

Not surprisingly, the liberal solution to obesity to is to take the responsibility away from the people who are eating the wrong foods and not getting enough exercise and put that responsibility on the shoulders of the companies selling the food. The liberal solution is not to eat less; the liberal solution is to sue. The liberal solution is to encourage people to eat whatever they want and then give them huge financial rewards for doing so. The liberal solution is—as always—to try to get something for nothing. The liberal solution is to just make things worse.

Conclusions

Throughout this chapter, we've touched on only a few of the countless examples of how liberal policies always seem to be based on the underlying and unspoken premise of trying to get something for nothing. Whether with regard to economics, race-relations, military strategy or even a person's own opinion of themselves, each and every thing liberals think, do or say seems to reflect nothing more than a superficial understanding of any given situation topped off with a hollow, yet aesthetically-pleasing plan on how to deal with it.

In the same way, we have also seen how so many liberal policies, rather than ever helping solve a problem, in fact do nothing less than serve to perpetuate it. Help the homeless by giving free booze to alcoholics. Prevent drug abuse by giving out free needles. Get people off of welfare by giving them every possible reason to stay on it. The reality is that none of these, or any other sort of "feel good" plan, can ever possibly do anything to help solve a problem—and none of them ever will.

So if liberal policies always seek to get something for nothing—and, in fact, only end up making things worse—how can we ever possibly hope to get anywhere in our society?

The answer is simple—we can only get somewhere by understanding that there is no free ride. By understanding that if we want something, we need to create it. Not out of thin air, not through big words, not through cute little names and certainly not through some sort of perpetual motion machine—but create it through work. Create it through investment. Create it through personal responsibility. Create it by understanding and addressing the root-cause of any and every problem. Create it not by doing what sounds fun or easy, but by doing that which is hard.

TEN

Statistical Manipulations

As many of us already know, liberals have no problem whatsoever saying anything they can get away with in order to justify their position on any particular issue. In some cases, they may talk about things that happened hundreds of years ago in order to defend policies they want to have put in place today. In other cases, they may simply make some sort of absurd claim that supports their position and then challenge you to prove them wrong. But interestingly, one of the things liberals seem to be doing more and more of is to actually turn to the facts in order to make their case—to quote some kind of statistic. And why not? How could anyone possibly argue with that? Numbers don't lie, right?—Wrong. Numbers can be made to lie.

The first thing to remember about any sort of statistic is that numbers alone rarely tell the whole story. Certainly numbers can be used to quantify the end result of just about any situation; but in most cases, they can never tell us anything about the *why*. They can never tell us anything about the *how*. Most important of all, they can never even tell us anything useful about what can be done to change the numbers themselves. Numbers, you see, focus exclusively on the effect and not the cause. And it is precisely this singular weakness that liberals have exploited so well in using them to help undermine our society.

Just take a look at the situation in Iraq. One of the most common numerical arguments liberals use to promote the myth of American incompetence is that Baghdad now has only six to eight hours of electricity a day, whereas before the U.S. came in and destroyed everything, it had more like eighteen to twenty. Of course, the situation here—as always—comes down to numbers simply quantifying the effect without providing any insight into the cause.

Nevertheless, despite what liberals may claim, the reason for the decrease in the amount of electricity available in Baghdad is not Halliburton, not American incompetence and certainly not because things were so much better under Saddam. The reason for the decrease in electricity is a combination of two key factors—the continuing sabotage of the distribution system by the insurgency (further reinforced by the Left constantly using these blackouts as way to attack the war) and, even more importantly, a dramatic shift in where the electricity actually goes[15].

Overall, even though Saddam Hussein destroyed much of the Iraqi infrastructure in order to create more headaches for the Bush Administration, thanks to the work of American contractors, there is considerably more electricity available now than there was before the war. The difference however, is that now parts of Baghdad and central Iraq get significantly less of it, while those much larger areas to north and south that had been continually starved of electricity under Saddam Hussein get significantly more. Add to this major reallocation of power the fact that terrorists are blowing up transmission towers at a rate of two a day, and we suddenly get a much clearer picture of the situation

---

15   Re-engineering Iraq by: Glenn Zorpette. IEEE (Institute of Electrical and Electronics Engineers) Spectrum. February, 2006.

than any meaningless number alone could ever provide.

Liberal Math

A December, 1992 article in Ebony Magazine with the title "Who Gets Welfare?" vehemently argued that whites, not blacks, collect the greatest share of public aid dollars. The article opens by telling us that "the image of the lazy Black welfare queen" is nothing but a "hideous stereotype." It then goes on to assert that "It is a myth that persists despite...studies showing that Whites overwhelmingly reap the lion's share of the dole."

Clearly, the point of this openly bigoted article is to supposedly enlighten people about this so-called myth, and the way the authors have chosen to do that is through the use of statistical manipulation. Obviously, they know that by using numbers to make their point, it becomes almost impossible to argue with their conclusions—unless of course, we realize that numbers alone don't tell the whole story. Since we do indeed realize that, the first thing we should do is dissect the information so that we are absolutely sure to understand the story.

Most people think of welfare as some sort of payment—either in the form of cash, free or subsidized housing, food stamps or Medicaid—which a healthy person below the retirement age gets from the government on a long term basis. On the other hand, most people think of social security as something an older person who has worked their entire lives gets in return for a lifetime of contribution into what is effectively a forced savings plan.

This article however, groups these two programs together and by doing so, concludes that "61 percent of welfare recipients are White, while 33 percent are Black." It also goes on to say "Social Security is the nation's largest welfare program..." and that of the 35.4 million people who receive retirement and disability checks, 88.7 percent are white and just 9.6 percent are black.

In other words, by simply including social security payments into the welfare equation, the authors can now claim that white people are almost twice as likely (61% vs. 33%) to collect welfare as blacks and can immediately alter the public perception of the underlying problem along the way.

Not surprisingly, the same article makes it a point to refer to the above statistics specifically regarding social security (i.e. 88.7% white vs. 9.6% black) as a "shocking disparity." However, the shock of this disparity quickly fades when we realize that blacks make up approximately 12% of the population whereas whites make up 75%. As a result, we would naturally expect that there would be about 6.3 times (i.e. 75% divided by 12%) as many white people above the age of 65 as there are black people and that the retirement benefits would necessarily reflect that fact.

Now liberals may say, "So what? There is still a disparity. After all, the ratio of whites to blacks that are receiving social security is 9.2 (i.e. 88.7% divided by 9.6%) and not 6.3—clearly, American society is still racist."

Well, not quite. Since the black population has grown so much faster than the white population over the past few generations, we would naturally expect that the percentage of black people above the age of 65 would be less than the percentage of whites when compared to the general population. Of course, a quick check of the census information confirms this to be the case.

As of the 2000 census, the number of whites over the age of 65 living in the US was 30.4 million, while the number of blacks over

65 was 2.8 million[16]. Now dividing 30.4 million by 2.8 million, we come up with a ratio of 10.9—even greater than the 9.2 number we would expect. All of a sudden the "shocking" 88.7% vs. 9.6% disparity is quite a bit less shocking isn't it?

But liberals know a good trick when they see it, so the article also makes it a point to distort reality by pointing out that 39.7 percent of the single mothers who receive some sort of government assistance are black while an almost equal number (38.1 percent) are white.

Now by dividing 38.1% by 39.7%, we see the ratios of white to black mothers receiving such aid is 0.96. However, the census data tells us there are 107.7 million white women living in the US, while there are only 18.2 million black women giving a ratio of 5.9. Dividing this population ratio of 5.9 by the recipient ratio of 0.96 gives us the ratio of 6.2—which tells us that black women are more than six times as likely as whites to be on this particular form of welfare. Apparently, the "hideous stereotype" actually does have some basis in reality after all.

Clearly, presenting numbers in certain ways provides a powerful tool for liberals' intent on distorting our perception of a problem. Unfortunately, all-too-often, these same liberals can manage to distort our perception even without having to juggle any numbers at all. In these cases, they simply present the information and claim the numbers speak for themselves. Of course, we already know that numbers alone can only quantify the effect and never actually address the cause—but this critical piece of logic never seems to deter a liberal. You see, liberals will simply present the numbers, invert or distort the true causality behind them, immediately demand special rights, monies and opportunities and viciously attack anyone who dares to look beyond the numbers to try to understand what is really going on.

---

16   The results of the 1990 census would be more appropriate, but were unavailable.

Just take a look at the article "How is the Criminal Justice System Racist?" from the well-known liberal website defendingjustice.org[17]. The article opens with the statement "Although many feel that the United States has overcome its racist history, the legacies of colonialism, slavery and racism still affect our policies and practices today."

The point of the article of course, is to try use numbers to prove racism. Some of the ways it does this include providing irrelevant publicly available statistical information such as:

- "Although Black Americans make up only 12.7% of the U.S. population, they make up 48.2% of adults in federal, state, or local prisons and jails;"

- "42.5% of prisoners on Death Row are Black;" and

- "Black males have a 32% chance of serving time in prison...; Hispanic males have a 17% chance; White males have a 6% chance.

Unfortunately, without a deeper understanding and analysis of the causality behind these statistics, the numbers alone prove absolutely nothing and certainly provide no evidence whatsoever of racism, colonialism or slavery. Yet, what do so-called "civil rights" groups repeatedly do with them? They use them as evidence of racism. They use them as evidence of discrimination. They use them as evidence of everything they could possibly get away with—except anything which

---

17   Among other things, their parent company (PRA) likes to make statements like: "Through skillful marketing the Right uses misleading terms such as "parental rights" and "personal responsibility" to oppose movements and organizations that promote tolerance and equality."

actually puts the responsibility of a crime on the person who committed it.

Worse yet, these same groups use these numbers to discourage the arrest or conviction of certain kinds of people for fear of retaliation in the form of harassment or some kind of frivolous lawsuit. In essence, they use them to give certain groups immunity from prosecution and therefore the freedom to commit any crime they want. Worst of all, they use them to protect those who are undermining our society and to punish those trying to preserve any kind of order.

The same abuse is true when it comes to discrimination in the workplace. Since numbers do not address the cause, numbers alone cannot ever possibly be proof of race, gender or any other form of discrimination. Yet, bad hiring decisions and millions of dollars of extortion payments are made each year by companies in order to avoid billions of dollars of legal settlements. The lesson: hire and promote people regardless of their abilities or let the statistic-mongers bankrupt your company.

Want more? Take a look at this little gem from the NOW website that supposedly provides irrefutable proof of discrimination in the workplace: "For every dollar earned by men, women on a whole earn 74 cents, African American women earn 63 cents and Latina women earn 57 cents." Horrible, isn't it? Unfortunately, it tells us nothing about why and again provides no proof whatsoever of any discrimination.

Interestingly however, what was written immediately after it could have provided some insight into the origin of those numbers if only these people actually cared enough to think it through: "According to the Census Bureau, only 25% of all doctors and lawyers are women. Less than 1% of auto mechanics are women. And women are only 8.4% of engineers."

In other words, it would seem that women tend to hold a smaller percentage of professional, higher-paying jobs. Unfortunately, those who are always trying to extract as much propaganda value as possible from these statistics refused to make the simple, logical and causal connection that if you work at lower paying jobs, you naturally make less money. Shocking, isn't it?

Of course, if these people really wanted to understand the situation, really wanted to help women and really wanted to add any value to society, they would try to dig one level deeper to find out the real reason why women tend to hold lower paying jobs. But then again, feminists have no interest in understanding causality because it only undermines the justification behind the handouts and preferences they so ferociously demand. They also have no interest whatsoever in allowing other people to try to understand the causality—just think back to what happened to Harvard President Lawrence Summers back in 2005 when he dared to even bring up the issue.

So what about the whole domestic violence charade and the billion dollar industry that it has turned into? Surely we have all heard feminists and other scam-artists intent on exploiting the worst of these situations for their own financial or political gain throw around statistics about how *a women is battered*[18] *every 15 seconds* and the resulting need to have special laws in place to protect them against the evils of men.

Yet, despite quoting (and almost always dramatically over-exaggerating) these figures, these same people are sure to make no mention whatsoever of a few other statistics—in particular, that according to a 1999 Department of Justice report, at least 39% of domestic violence

---

18   Note the term—battered. Yet another trick of liberal statistics: group as many things as possible—no matter how petty they may be—under one umbrella and then use the harshest high-impact word you can to describe them. And if someone dares to want to understand the specifics of what actually happened—just scream in their face as loud as you possibly can.

is actually committed *by* women and that in some States one-quarter to one-third of those arrested for acts of domestic violence *are* women. Taking into account the fact that men are considerably less likely (five times less likely according to research by the respected family violence researcher M.A. Strauss in 1990) to call the police if their wife pushes them or throws something at them, and all of a sudden we start to see the real picture[19].

Unfortunately, feminists can never stand to deal with the reality of anything, so their typical response (after throwing a tirade, of course) is to insist that women batters were "only acting in self-defense". Of course, this justification completely flies in the face of their own prime directive: *There is NO excuse for Domestic Violence.* No excuse—except being a woman, that is.

But what about all the statistical studies that show how sports promote violence against women? Simple—throw them out. No matter what evidence any scowling Berkeley post-doc may try to present, there is absolutely no causality whatsoever to back up the conclusion that sports promotes violence and any carefully-tailored statistics used to do so reflect nothing more than a loose, irrelevant and very weak underlying correlation[20]. In other words—they mean absolutely nothing.

---

19   There are several books which present a more rational and factual accurate analysis of the realities of domestic violence including *Abused men: The hidden side of domestic violence* by Philip Cook; *When she was bad: Violent women and the myth of innocence* by Patricia Pearson; *Who stole feminism: How women have betrayed women* by Christina Hoff Sommers; and *The myth of male power* by Warren Farrell.

20   See Chapter 7 for more information on Causality, Correlation and Coincidence.

Hate Crimes

Perhaps the most vile of all liberal creations is the concept of the hate crime. You see, liberals—despite every vociferous, superficial and manipulative claim to the contrary—do not for one moment believe the law should be applied equally to everyone. No, liberals believe the law is simply nothing more than another tool to be used for their own personal and political gain and to guarantee them special rights, exemptions from responsibility and absolute freedom to do whatever they want to other people—all at someone else's expense.

As such, the very concept of the hate crime represents the worst of what liberalism is really about and is so absolutely hideous because it embodies so many of the other tools and methodologies described throughout this book including Promote and Exploit Divisiveness, Bad Competition, Groupdividual, Implicit Assumptions, The Perpetual Motion Machine, Negative, Asymmetry and Guises into one disgusting, systematic and ever increasing bigotry used to create a new caste system in which certain people are permanently demoted to the rank of a second class citizen based on nothing more than race and gender. And one of the most powerful tools liberals use to justify this absolute abomination of justice is the manipulation and endless repetition of a small group of carefully selected statistical data.

Since the passage of the Hate Crimes Statistics Act of 1990, the FBI has been keeping track of just how many incidents can be classified in this absurd way. Now, armed with this information, liberals are relentlessly using these numbers to stir everyone into frenzy. However, a closer look at the most recent numbers (i.e. 2004) will certainly be enlightening as the scope of this so-called "epidemic."

The first thing to note is that in 2004, there were an estimated

1,367,009 violent crimes nationwide. The second thing to note is that in this same year, there were 9,528 victims of incidents classified as hate crimes by the FBI[21]. Furthermore, of these 9,528 incidents, only 5,642 were crimes against persons (as opposed to property). However, of these 5,642 crimes against persons, 2,827 were classified as "intimidation," which generally means calling someone a bad name. The net result is that only 2,815 of these situations actually involved any physical contact.

However, in 1,750 of these cases, the physical contact was classified as "simple assault," which generally means pushing someone away from you. Taking these non-events out of the equation, we are left with reality that despite every effort by liberals to lower to bar on what ultimately makes the list, only 1,065 out of the 1,367,009 violent crimes in the US—less than 0.08%—can even be considered as hate-crimes.

But since we all know that hate crimes only matter when they are committed against homosexuals or minorities—and in all too many instances, they are not even reported as such unless they are—we should take a quick look at some of those figures.

According to Table 4 of the FBI's 2004 hate crime report, there were exactly 113 cases of violent hate crimes committed against homosexual men—i.e. less than 0.008% of all violent crime. Furthermore, if we make the assumption that whites commit the same ratio[22] of violent hate crimes against homosexuals as they do of all so-called hate crimes against homosexuals, we see that at the end of the day, the evil heterosexual white male actually committed only 50 violent hate crimes against homosexual men in all of 2004. Add to this, the

---

21   And this is based on the ASSUMPTION that all of these crimes were committed based on some kind of race, gender or other bias. There should be no doubt that a more realistic analysis of the causality would prove that in many of these cases, there was actually some other reason.

22   44% based on Table 5 (376 out of 855 offenses).

fascinating fact that when a Hispanic commits a hate crime, for some reason he is suddenly counted as being white, and you start to see the real picture.

Of course, in the rare instance when one of these violent crimes does occur, the propaganda value is enormous and you can be sure the story will immediately end up as front page news. A perfect example would be the situation in New Bedford, Massachusetts where an 18 year-old white male attacked three people in a gay bar on February 2, 2006.

Not surprisingly, House Democratic Leader Nancy Pelosi—always quick to exploit every situation for her own benefit—immediately released the following statement regarding the need to enact a federal hate crimes prevention law:

> "As the brutal attack in New Bedford clearly indicates, hate crimes persist in our country, and federal hate crimes prevention legislation is long overdue... Hate crimes have no place in America. All Americans have a fundamental right to feel safe in their communities - regardless of their sexual orientation, gender identity, race, color, religion, national origin, gender, or disability... We must act to end hate crimes. We must honor this nation's commitment to the ideals of justice, equality and opportunity."

This statement, like all other liberal statements on hate crimes, is a perfect example of only one vile thing—liberal propaganda at its finest.

Conclusions

As we have seen, liberals love to quote statistics. Unfortunately, as we have also seen, the statistics they tend to use are either wrong, irrelevant, skewed by some inaccurate measurement or intentionally biased in order to help justify their position on any given issue.

Still, there is no doubt that liberals will continue to inundate us with these sort of meaningless numbers in order to try to get whatever it is they want, and one of the most subtle techniques for doing this is through the use of polling.

You see, one of the best ways to get someone to think or act in a certain way is for them to know other people are thinking or acting in that particular way. Similarly, one of the best ways to get someone not to think or act in a certain way is to make them feel as though they would somehow be wrong in doing so. It all comes down to the same things—peer pressure, groupthink, fear of being different, intimidation and coercion—and statistics are a phenomenal resource for liberals to use in all of these areas.

A simple example of this sort of mind game would be the widely publicized Gallup Poll conducted during the period of February 9th to February 12th of 2006 which asked the question: *Do you approve or disapprove of the way George W. Bush is handling his job as president?*

The response to this survey was 39% approve, 56% disapprove and 4% had no opinion. Certainly these numbers are not great—but what do they really mean? How many of these people would not approve regardless of what Bush does (i.e. the Bush haters)? How many of these people are not happy with things the President has no control over, yet still blame him for? How many of these people have no idea of the complexities involved in the situations the country faces and that to preserve any kind of future, there are often sacrifices that need to be made in the present? How many of these people think Bush is too conservative? And most important of all—how many think he is too liberal.

Clearly, when looked at from this perspective, a 39% approval rating—though by no means, anything to be proud of—does not provide any insight whatsoever as to what the problems or the solutions really are. It does, however, give liberals an incredibly valuable psychological tool they can use to get people to question whatever support they may have for the President or the Republican Party.

By the way, another less publicized Gallup poll conducted around the same time found just 27% of Americans approved of the way Congress was handling its job. By comparison, Bush looks like a genius.

ELEVEN

Negative

One of the most powerful tools liberals use to consistently undermine our society is the endless chorus of negativity that dominates everything they say. Take a look at just about any article in a liberal newspaper—the focus is always on the negative. Listen to a liberal politician make a statement—the focus is always on the negative. Listen to liberals try to justify their position on any issue whatsoever—the focus is always on the negative.

Remember the whole Abu Gharib prison scandal? From the moment the story broke, liberals were literally falling all over themselves to take a series of isolated incidents and replay them over and over again in the most negative ways imaginable. Every day the same pictures on the cover of the New York Times. Every day more liberals mouthing off about the evils of torture. Every day more liberals lecturing about the evils of our military. Every day more liberals salivating as they tried to portray the United States in the worst way possible—all while completely ignoring the beheadings going in Iraq on at exactly the same time.

Not that their actions should come as any surprise. After all, no liberal would ever want to put anything the military does in any sort of context. Take embedded journalists, for example. They follow soldiers around war-zones every day, videotaping everything they do, hoping for that one mistake, that one moment of film, that one little thing they can harp on to make the military look bad and ruin the life of someone who had already given more to society by the time they were twenty years old than all the journalists trying to crucify him ever will.

The same is true for the police. Thanks to liberals, even the slightest mistake becomes the focus of national attention, completely negating everything that a particular officer—or the thousands of others around the country—has ever done. Never any mention of the positive; only the negative.

Ever listen to Howard Dean make a speech? What about Hillary Clinton? Chuck Schumer? Barbara Boxer? Al Gore? How about someone from the ACLU? MoveOn.org? Greenpeace? What about PETA? GLAAD? The NAACP? Is their focus ever on the positive of what they can do—or is it on the negative of everything else? We know the answer.

Every sound bite. Every statement. Every rally. Every cause. Every justification. Nothing is ever appreciated. Nothing is ever respected. Nothing is ever good enough. In fact, nothing is ever good at all—unless is happens to be completely in line with the twisted agenda of the left.

Rose Colored Glasses?

Liberals like to think of themselves as idealists and are quick to tell everyone how they tend to look at the world through rose-colored glasses. Well, let's take a look through those glasses and try to decide for ourselves what color they really are.

On November 17, 2005, US Congressman John P. Murtha (D-PA) issued the following statement about the situation in Iraq:

> The war in Iraq is not going as advertised. It is a flawed policy wrapped in illusion... Our military is suffering. The future of our country is at risk...
>
> Many say that the Army is broken... Recruitment is down, even as our military has lowered its standards... Much of our ground equipment is worn out...
>
> Oil production and energy production are below pre-war levels... Clean water is scarce... Since the revelations at Abu Ghraib, American casualties have doubled. An annual State Department report in 2004 indicated a sharp increase in global terrorism...
>
> ... All of Iraq must know that Iraq is free. Free from United States occupation...

Of course, Republicans were not very happy with this barrage of negativity (which could have easily been said in a much more constructive way—if being constructive had actually been the goal) and a few of them had the nerve to voice their concerns. But Democrats love to criticize and absolutely hate to be criticized, so they naturally did what they do best—they attacked with more negativity.

On November 18th, John Kerry spoke on the Senate Floor to "respond to the sickening attacks on decorated veteran Rep. Jack Murtha:"

> "Mr. President... I am not going to stand for a swift boat attack strategy against Jack Murtha.
>
> "It disgusts me that a bunch of guys who have

never put on the uniform of their country venomously turn their guns on a marine who served his country heroically in Vietnam and has been serving heroically in Congress ever since...

"Dennis Hastert...who never served, called Jack Murtha a coward and accused him of wanting to cut and run... Jack Murtha didn't cut and run when his courage in combat earned him a Bronze Star, and his voice should be heard, not silenced by those who still today cut and run from the truth.

"Just a day after Dick Cheney, who had 5 deferments from Vietnam, accused Democrats of being unpatriotic—the White House accused Jack Murtha of surrendering. Jack Murtha...doesn't know how to surrender - not to enemy combatants, and not to politicians in Washington...

It doesn't matter who you are... this administration will go to any lengths to crush any dissent.

"Once again, they're engaged in the lowest form of smear and fear politics ... They're afraid to debate a decorated veteran who lives and breathes the concerns of our troops, not the empty slogans of an Administration that sent our brave troops to war without body armor...

Not that John Kerry's negativity should come as any surprise, mind you—after all, his entire 2004 Presidential campaign was fueled by negativity. Thankfully however, he never knew when to let up, because if he did he might actually be President right now. But when Osama Bin Laden released a tape threatening America just days before the election, Kerry tried to capitalize on it in the only way he knows how—

by being negative. His comment of "...Osama bin Laden and Al-Qaida were cornered in the mountains of Tora Bora, and it was wrong to *outsource* (his spoken emphasis) the job of capturing them to Afghan warlords...," deservedly turned off a lot of voters. Instead of telling the American people what he was going to do as commander-in-chief, Kerry chose to go negative. No doubt this made people cringe at the thought of a weasel like him being President and very possibly cost him the election.

Unfortunately, John Kerry—like all liberals—knows of no other way of communicating as is obvious from a couple of excerpts from his November 2, 2005 eulogy for Rosa Parks: "For Rosa Parks and for America, it is our own time to answer 'no' to those who would deny or degrade equality in the name of states' rights, or with the false claim that our history is color blind," and "It is our time to demand that every vote be counted and no voters be discounted because of the color of their skin—for Rosa Parks and for our country." Apparently, he forgot to mention the most important "for" of all—for himself.

But let's stop focusing on Kerry. Instead, let's take a look at what Democratic Leader Nancy Pelosi had to say about Arnold Schwarzenegger being elected governor of California back in 2003. That night, she told reporters that the California recall "is a sad night for our country... Now we have the cavalier notion that a recall without just cause is okay." But apparently that non sequitur was not negative enough, so she immediately threw a hissy fit and added another, "I think the message in California is a message for President Bush: "Stop your reckless economic policies that are resulting in record joblessness... and record deficits.""

A few days later, Pelosi was finally able to think a little more clearly (given the inherent limitations she apparently has to work with) and at least had a coherent focus to her negativity. At that point, she issued the following statement (supposedly about the recall):

> "This election was about jobs and the economy. Among the main arguments used against Governor Davis was that he inherited record surpluses and turned them into record deficits and presided over a weak economy that has lost jobs.
>
> "President Bush should take heed of that message. The American people are anxious about the economy and increasingly angry at his failed leadership. The President's reckless economic policies have resulted in record joblessness and record deficits..."

Unfortunately, this is just a small sample of the sort of things we have come to expect from the House Democratic leader. Never anything of substance. Never anything useful about any issues. Never anything constructive in any way other than for her own benefit. Nothing but the pretense of caring about an issue and abusing her political platform to attack others with an endless barrage of negativity.

Fortunately however, Pelosi is the not the leader of the entire Democratic Party, only of those Democrats in the House of Representatives. Given this situation, maybe we can find some useful leadership elsewhere, so let's take a look at some of what Senate Democrat leader Harry Reid has to say.

According to his website, Reid released a statement on December 19, 2005 titled *This Congress's Corruption Has Gone Too Far*: "The Republican Congress has put their special interest friends at the top of their agenda this week as they rush to finish business before the holiday break. While they work to ensure big oil, the drug industry and the banks get everything on their wish list, middle-class Americans are learning just what it means to have a corrupt Congress abusing their power..."

Not off to a good start, are we? In fact, looking at the other press releases on his website, it seems like there is not much a difference between him and Pelosi after all. Here are just a few of his headlines:

- 12/16/05—Reid: Protecting Our Borders Should Not Include Demonizing Immigrants

- 12/15/05—Senate Democratic Leaders Call on Bush to Place Interests of American Families Ahead of Tax Breaks for Special Interests and Multi-Millionaires

- 12/14/05—Reid Pide A Frist Que Actúe Para Proteger A Los Estadounidenses De La Gripe Aviaria

- 12/14/05—Debemos Dar Acceso A Educación Universitaria A Más Estudiantes, Dice Reid Líder Demócrata Anuncia Su Continuo Apoyo A La Ley Dream

- 12/14/05—President Disregards Advice of 41 Senators, Fails to Level with the American People

- 12/13/05—Reid y Durbin Piden que se Vuelva a Convocar a Grupo de Trabajo de Seis Miembros que Investiga Inteligencia Antes de la Guerra

- 12/09/05—Capacidades De Liderazgo De Menendez Serán Gran Contribución Para El Senado, Dice Reid

- 12/06/05—Líderes Demócratas Le Piden A Bush Brindar Una Estrategia Real Para El Éxito En Irak

- 12/05/05—Declaración de Reid sobre las Calificaciones de la Comisión del 9/11

- 12/05/05—Reid Pide al Departamento de Justicia que Proteja el Derecho al Voto, no a la Mayoría Republicana

- 12/05/05—Bush Debería Ser Congruente Con Sus Palabras, Dice Reid

- 12/02/05-- Reid: Hay Más Trabajo Por Hacer Por Las Familias De Los Estados Unidos

Now don't let the fact that a US Senator has so many of his press releases issued and posted in Spanish bother you. After all, Reid really cares about the Mexican—I mean the American—people. Just take a look at his October 31, 2005 statement regarding the nomination of Judge Samuel Alito to the United States Supreme Court:

> The nomination of Judge Alito requires an especially long hard look by the Senate because of what happened last week to Harriet Miers.
>
> Conservative activists forced Miers to withdraw from consideration for this same Supreme Court seat because she was not radical enough for them. Now the Senate needs to find out if the man replacing Miers is too radical for the American people...
>
> The President has chosen a man to replace Sandra Day O'Connor, one of only two women on the Court. For the third time, he has declined to make history by nominating the first Hispanic to the Court...President

Bush would leave the Supreme Court looking less like
America and more like an old boys club...

Okay, okay. So the Democratic leaders in both the House and the
Senate are obsessed with negativity—but that does not reflect the party
itself, does it? To get a better feel for them, we should probably take a
look at the man who does represent the Democrats—the Chairman of
the DNC, Mr. Howard Dean.

You know, I can't help but wonder why he was elected to that
position. Let me take a look back to see if I can find out. Oh, here it is.

In the days before the election, Dean was telling Democrats
gathered at a Manhattan hotel that "I hate the Republicans and everything
they stand for." Apparently, that was all they needed to hear.

Dean, Kerry, Pelosi and Reid—some pretty high profile
Democrats, right? But who are we missing? God, there are just so many
to choose from. I know—let's take a look at another liberal who was a
hair's breadth away from the Presidency—Al Gore.

According to a May 27, 2004 article on Fox News website titled
Gore Demands Bush Team Resignations, Al Gore, screaming as usual, attacked
the Bush administration policy on Iraq with a barrage of negativity:

> "How dare they subject us to such dishonor
> and disgrace! How dare they drag the good name of
> the United States of America through the mud of
> Saddam Hussein's torture prison! I am calling today
> for...the immediate resignations of those...responsible
> for creating the catastrophe we are facing in Iraq..."

Gore also claimed that the soldiers who were abusing prisoners
"were clearly forced to wade into a moral cesspool designed by the Bush

White House..." and added that "The worst still lies ahead."

But enough about liberal politicians. What negativity lurks within the minds of other kinds of liberals? Well, we can start with a statement prominently featured on the website of the NAACP: "Today we face a renewed effort as the forces of racism and retrogression in America are again on the rise. Many of the hard-earned civil rights gains of the past three decades are under assault." So much for liberals and race relations.

Unfortunately, when it comes to gender related issues, liberals are just as negative. Take a look at some of what was said at a recent NOW rally in this September 2, 2004 article—*Feminists Compare Bush's 2000 Election Victory To 'Savage Rape'*—by Marc Morano published on CNSNews.com where so-called poets were still fuming over Bush's "stealing" the 2000 Presidential election:

> "Imagine a way to erase that night four years
> ago when you (President Bush) savagely raped every
> pandemic woman over and over with each vote you got,
> a thrust with each state you stole," (Molly) Birnbaum
> said... "A smack with each bill you passed, a tear with
> each right you took until you left me disenfranchised
> with hands shackled and voice restrained...

Does all this negativity (not to mention raging immaturity) make you want to vomit? Well, here are a few more things to consider, like this excerpt from the December 16, 2005 article *University Administrator Declares Christmas 'Forbidden'* also from CNSNews.com.

> An administrator at California State University,
> Sacramento has banned decorations pertaining to

Christmas and the 4th of July, among other holidays, from her office because they represent "religious discrimination" and "ethnic insensitivity...

Nice, huh? Well, how about the December 19, 2005 cover of The New Yorker magazine which featured a drawing of a sad soldier sitting in Iraq counting out the days by marking up a wall with dozens of 5-symbol slashes in the shape of a Christmas tree? With this one picture, liberals got to attack both Bush and Christmas with the added bonus of making our soldiers out to be sad-sack buffoons sitting out in the desert waiting to come home to be spat on. What a great booster for military morale. But then, what can you expected from the sort of people who are always focused on the negative.

No Good Deed Goes Unpunished

On December 15, 2005, the New York Times broke the story about the Bush Administration conducting certain wiretap operations for national security purposes without getting a warrant for them. Liberals were thrilled—now they had something they could really focus their negativity on. The politicians went wild. The media went wild. The people went wild. Most of all, the ACLU went wild and, among other things, ran a full-page ad in the December 22, 2005 edition of The New York Times with a picture of President Bush juxtaposed against a picture of Richard Nixon. The message was simple: Nixon was a criminal and Bush should be considered to be one too.

Of course, only a liberal could compare wiretapping for national security purposes after thousands of Americans were killed by terrorists, with wiretapping for political purposes. By the way, as far as I know, there was no full page ad by the ACLU calling for an investigation into Clinton for being above the law when it came to multiple charges of sexual harassment or the felony crime of lying under oath. In the same way, there were no ads about Cynthia McKinney not being above the law when she assaulted a police officer and justified it through her completely asinine accusations of racism.

But when it came to the situation with Bush, not only did they run the ad, but the ACLU then demanded records from the NSA and other agencies in connection with the domestic spying that was approved by the president. Just great—take all national security issues and make them matters of public record. Let terrorists, collaborators and sympathizers know they are being watched so they can adjust their behavior accordingly. After all, we're Americans; we don't want to ruin their chances of success in the next attack, do we?

Furthermore, once the Administration announced it would launch an investigation to find out who leaked the information about the program to the press, the ACLU went negative again.

On December 30, 2005 they slammed the Department of Justice investigation and released a statement by their Executive Director Anthony D. Romero:

> President Bush broke the law and lied to the American people when he unilaterally authorized secret wiretaps of U.S. citizens. But rather than focus on this constitutional crisis, Attorney General Gonzales is cracking down on critics of his friend and boss...
>
> To avoid further charges of cronyism, Attorney General Gonzales should call off the investigation...

Right—call off the investigation before the spies Clinton planted in the organization get discovered.

Negative. Negative. Negative. No gratitude for being kept safe for four years. No balance. No discussion of the complexities of the situation. Not even any appearance of trying to do something useful by talking about changing policies going forward—only focusing on the negative as often as humanly possible.

Need more? Just take a look at the December 28, 2005 piece in the New York Times by the well-known liberal columnist Maureen Dowd. The story opens with, "We start the new year with the same old fear: Dick Cheney." It then rambles on with one witless statement after another attacking both Cheney and Donald Rumsfeld including accusations about "steroid-infused power grabs," and about the "most ridiculously pumped-up presidency ever." The piece ends with "Checks, balances, warrants, civil liberties—they're all so 20th century..."

Pretty bitter, huh? Well, that should come as no surprise—just look at the titles of the other columns she had written about Bush and Cheney over the previous month:

- December 21, 2005—The Squires of Surveillance

- December 17, 2005—Hot Monkey Love: President Bush might want to think twice before resurrecting his cowboy routine. He might conjure up images of Bushback Mountain.

- December 14, 2005—W. Won't Read This: Never ask a guy who's in a bubble if he's in a bubble.

- December 3, 2005—W's Head In the Sand: The Bush warriors are so deluded they're even faking their fakery.

- November 30, 2005—The Autumn Of the Patriarchy: Inside the vice president's bunker mentality.

So hateful. So bitter. So negative. But then again, what else would you expect from a liberal—especially one who would actually be proud of publishing a book with the title *Are Men Necessary?*

All this negativity despite the fact that—thanks to the actions of the Bush Administration—there have been no attacks on American soil in nearly five years since 9/11. Five years within which there have been multiple attacks in the subways of London, an attack that killed hundreds of people on a Madrid train, dozens of suicide bombings in Israel, hundreds of Muslims blowing up other Muslims all over Iraq just to get the attention of the American media, thousands of Muslims torching thousands of cars in France and, of course, the occasional bombings in Bali, Indonesia and elsewhere. But not a single terrorist act on American soil—not even a paper cut.

Still liberals focus on the negative. Still they have to attack. Still they have to criticize. Still they have to scream about imaginary violations of rights and about fascism, war-mongering and imperialism. Still no sign of gratitude or any acknowledgement whatsoever of their own responsibilities. Still nothing—except negative, negative, negative.

Conclusions

So there you have it—liberal viewpoints and statements on just about everything. Pretty depressing isn't it?

But don't get me wrong—I'm not saying that liberals have a monopoly on negativity; they certainly do not. After all, conservatives could be quite negative themselves when it comes to things like terrorists flying airplanes into buildings, twelve million illegal aliens living in the United States and any sort of institutional or government-mandated discrimination that elevates certain people at the expense of others.

On the other hand, liberals tend to be negative about much more important things like having to spend an extra ten seconds going through security at the airport, hearing someone say "Merry Christmas" or seeing the US come out on top in any sort of military situation.

To liberals, negativity is so ingrained in their psyche that they have no choice but to behave the way they do. No wonder they are always so focused on victimhood and victimization. Instead of focusing on the freedoms of this country, they focus on what they can't do—like avoid all possible forms of responsibility all the time. They focus on slavery, on oppression, on evil corporations and doom and gloom. They always focus on how to make something wrong.

Not surprisingly, liberals are the first to complain about the county's dependence on foreign oil—and the first to obstruct any way to eliminate that dependency. Just take a look at nuclear energy—or at least at what is left of it. The fact is, there has not been a new reactor authorized in the US since the mid-seventies. Why?—Liberals, or more specifically, liberal negativity.

Doom and gloom. Doom and gloom. Doom and gloom. Radioactive fish. Children with three heads. Pictures of burn victims

131

from Hiroshima. The reality is nuclear energy has not killed a single person in the United States and it is doubtful whether it has ever caused any sort of long-term health problems for anyone either.

But liberals don't care about reality; they only care about negativity—especially when that negativity can be used to obstruct any sort of progress. So liberals protested nuclear energy to death and—for all practical purposes—that option to reduce our dependency on foreign oil is pretty much off the table.

But what about hydroelectric power? Well that's no good either because of the effect on the environment. What if it tarnishes the natural beauty of a place nobody ever goes to? What if it affects the mating habits of some bird no one's every heard of? Worse yet—what if someone actually makes money building the dam or from the electricity that it generates? Liberals can't have that.

Well there is always coal, right? Wrong—too dirty for liberals. Too old fashioned. Too quaint. Too offensive in its odor. And oh, those filthy coal miners.

Okay, forget nuclear power. Forget hydroelectric. Forget coal. How about we actually make use of our own domestic reserves?— DON'T EVEN THINK ABOUT IT!

Remember all the screaming liberals did about the Alaska Pipeline back in the 1970's? All the doom and gloom. All the crying about the melting of the permafrost, the ruining of the environment and how hard it would be for the Caribou to get around. And no matter what solutions were presented to these problems, they still were not good enough for the liberals.

How many years did their negativity end up adding to the project? How many billions of dollars? And like all liberal predictions, did any of it ever come true? Of course not.

Now given that situation, you would think liberals would have learned their lesson—that these companies know what they are doing and they will be held accountable for any problems. So shut up and go away. But does any of this ever happen? Never.

Now, in 2006 we are going through the exact same thing with ANWR (Arctic National Wildlife Refuge) drilling. The same complaints. The same outrage. The same rhetoric. The same negativity.

So when it comes to oil, liberals are negative. When it comes to no oil, liberals are negative. Doom and gloom and no solution—except driving around in little electric cars with vanity plates meant to tell you what great people they are. Ever hear a liberal scream *No blood for Oil*? Well, thanks to them, the reality of the situation is "More blood for oil."

Liberals—they just can't help but be negative.

The evils of corporations. The evils of Christianity. The imperialistic appetite of the United States, which rebuilt Germany and Japan—the same counties that had just tried to drive us into extinction—into economic superpowers. The same country that spends hundreds of billion of dollars each year paying the Arab world for oil that we could have just as easily taken by force. Will it ever end? Don't count on it. I mean, for God's sake—even liberal bumper stickers are negative.

Drive around San Francisco sometime. Drive around and see for yourself just what liberals have on their minds. Here are just a few of the liberal bumper stickers I've seen around here:

- Republican't
- Hatred is NOT a Family Value
- Please Don't Start WWIII
- Doing My Best to Piss Off the Religious Right
- Feminism is the Radical Notion that Women are Human Beings

- Keep Your Laws Off My Body!
- Dick + Bush = Screwed
- Great Spirits Have Always Faced Violent Opposition From Mediocre Minds
- One Nation Under Surveillance
- Got Rights?
- Bush Lied, People Died
- Regime Change Begins At Home
- Somewhere in Texas There's A Village Missing An Idiot
- Who Would Jesus Bomb?
- SILLY ME: I Thought We Were Living In a Democracy
- The War To End All Peace: Operation Enduring Terror
- Don't Steal. The Government Hates Competition
- I Think, Therefore I Don't Listen to Rush Limbaugh
- Well Behaved Women Seldom Make History
- Sorry I Missed Church, I've Been Busy Practicing Witchcraft and Becoming A Lesbian
- If you're not OUTRAGED you're not paying attention
- Congress gave huge tax cuts to the rich and all I got was this lousy bumper sticker

Of course, you could always contrast these idiotic statements with conservative bumper stickers—which are usually an American Flag or a yellow ribbon engraved with the words *Support Our Troops.*

Clearly, liberals can't stand success. They can't stand structure. They can't stand seeing anyone or anything ever being successful. The only thing they can stand is being negative—and that negativity gives them an incredibly powerful tool in their never ending quest to destroy our country.

TWELVE

Hostile Foreign Governments

One of Albert Einstein's favorite ways to find the solution to a problem he was working on was to do what in German is called a *Gedankenexperiment*—a thought experiment. What this means essentially, is to think through a situation as logically and as objectively as possible in order to try to gain some new insights into it beyond what is already known. Since this certainly sounds like an interesting approach to me, why don't we go ahead and try it?

Suppose a foreign government wanted to undermine the United States for some reason, what would be the best way for them to go about doing it? Certainly not militarily, as there is clearly no possible way any country could ever spend enough to win an all out war against us. Even in the unlikely situation that they were to somehow come close—or even to seriously threaten any of our national interests—any such conflict would ultimately go nuclear. In that case, the best possible outcome for them would be some form of mutually assured destruction. Clearly, taking on the US in a direct military conflict is not a very viable option.

Now if these governments are unable to beat us militarily, what other options do they have? Certainly, another approach they could use might be to try to beat us economically—by destroying our manufacturing base, for example. As it turns out, some of them—China, in particular—are actively working on trying to do just that. But any sort of economic attack like this takes decades to show any meaningful result and quite a bit can happen in that amount of time[23].

So if these governments cannot beat us militarily and they can't beat us economically (at least not in the short term), they really have only one other option at their disposal. That option is destroy us from within. That option is to use our own freedoms against us. That option is create, encourage and exploit every possible form of propaganda known to man to make the American people think and act in ways that are contrary to the best interests of this country. And there is no better way to spread this sort of anti-American propaganda than through the conduit of the American Left.

So is this partnership with liberals a hypothetical scenario, or could something like this really be happening? Since we know that the United States (through the CIA and other means) has often tried to undermine the governments of other countries—Iran, Iraq, Libya, Cuba, Nicaragua and so on—why would there be any doubt whatsoever that other countries would be trying to do the same thing to us?

Certainly, it would be fair to assume that other governments—especially those run by dictators, fascists, communists or Muslim fanatics who want nothing more than to stay in power at all costs—tend to act in their own best interests. So given this assumption, why should we believe a country like Iran would sit around twiddling its thumbs as we actively try to undermine their nuclear program and have their fanatical

---

23   For one, assuming capitalism was allowed to run its course, the United States would likely find ways to improve manufacturing efficiencies or develop new and better technologies to counter any such assault. However, even if this didn't happen, the government could always defend against this sort of attack by putting tariffs in place to significantly reduce the import of any foreign products.

HOSTILE FOREIGN GOVERNMENTS

Mullahs removed from power? Why should we think Hugo Chavez is naïve enough to care only about what people in Venezuela think of him? Why should we think Castro's only export is cigars? And why should we think countries like China and North Korea are not watching CNN twenty-four hours a day looking for any kind of weaknesses they could exploit in order to give them the opportunity to do whatever they want without any interference from us?

There is only one answer to all these questions. That answer is—we shouldn't.

Symbiotic Parasites

In nature, when two different organisms work together for their mutual benefit, they are generally considered to have what is known as a symbiotic relationship. On the other hand, when one an organism survives by extracting resources from another and slowly kills it in the process, we have what is known as a parasitic relationship.

Since the Left tends to work so closely with foreign governments—or any other international organization hostile to the interests of the United States—clearly they share a symbiotic relationship. Since these groups also seem to share the common goal of undermining the United States in every way they possibly can, we can also consider them to be nothing more than parasites. Given this situation, the overall relationship between liberals and these groups can be best described by a new term—*Symbiotic Parasites*.

So how do these Symbiotic Parasites operate? Simple—by spreading propaganda and fostering internal discord. And what mechanisms would they use to further these efforts? You guessed it—each and every one of the tools and methodologies described

139

throughout this book. Foreign governments provide the propaganda and the money, and the America-hating liberals do the rest.

Any country in the world could simply funnel ten million dollars—a fraction of the cost of a single fighter jet—to a couple of dozen purported peace groups, environmental groups, animal rights groups and civil liberty unions and do more damage to us than that country's entire military combined. It would be—and is—the ultimate return on investment for them. Finance the Left, and let them do the rest. Let them protest the government. Let them constrain the military. Let them stir up civil disobedience. Let them undermine, sabotage, attack and destroy. Let them do everything you want them to do—all while you sit back and smile.

When was the last time the Left supported any sort of foreign policy that a country like North Korea didn't like? When was the last time the Left supported a Presidential candidate that a terrorist like Osama Bin Laden didn't like? When was the last time the Left did anything contrary to the interests of any country other than the United States? All these questions have the exact same answer—never.

When it comes to issues of national security—and of national survival—both liberals and hostile foreign governments always want the exact same things. These governments want us to put the worst possible people in power. They want the weakest people we have negotiating with them—which is exactly why there was so much opposition to Bush's selection of John Bolton as ambassador to the UN. They want appeasers and America-haters and people who don't want to rock the boat at every level of government. They want politicians willing to look the other way and who stand ready to make back-room deals for their own short-term benefit while sacrificing the long-term interests of this country. Simply put, they want liberals.

They want there to be no Patriot Act. They want no government wiretaps of calls from known terrorists into the United States. They want no money to be spent on new weapons programs. They want nothing that could help us protect ourselves in any way, shape or form.

These governments want nothing more than to breed divisiveness within this country by using our own openness, our own tolerance, our own diversity and our own freedoms against us—all while claiming none of these things exist. They want nothing more than to perpetuate problems, discourage military spending, promote outsourcing, flood our markets with their goods and drive our manufacturing base into extinction. And on top of it all, they want those who actually care about the future of this country to be fighting so many battles at home that they don't have the time or the willpower to fight any battles—military or otherwise—against them.

Take a look at North Korea, which constantly makes all sorts of noise about how the US is planning an invasion and then turns around and threatens us with "a rain of fire" if we try. They continually antagonize the US—not for the purpose of directly deterring any military action mind you, but to drive the American Left into a frenzy and let them do the rest.

The Left is their leverage; their puppet. The left is their ace-in-the-hole. The Left is their dream. After all, how could the US possibly do anything about a North Korean nuclear program when liberals in the House, liberals in the Senate, liberals in the media and liberals screaming in the streets are actively undermining us every step of the way? *We're acting too late! We're acting too early! We're acting alone! Another quagmire! Bush provoked them! Why can't they have the same weapons we do! No blood for kimchi! Impeach Bush!*

The same thing is true in Iran. All they need to do in order to make themselves untouchable is to take a look over the border into Iraq and find a way to leverage that situation for their own benefit.

And the best way to do that—knowing they can always count on their partners here in the States—is to simply to send a few dozen operatives into Iraq every couple of weeks to blow up mosques, kill civilians and target American soldiers with suicide bombs. Of course, in a real war this sort of pitter-patter would be absolutely meaningless and would be crushed in a matter of days; unfortunately, the US is now engaged in a media war—and the American media is more than happy to glorify every problem, ignore every victory and spin every situation to make it seem as though the US is caught in a quagmire.

Worse yet, just as it was in Vietnam, this dream of the Left could easily become a self-serving prophecy simply by allowing the enemy to spread their message, wear down the American people and keep the liberal enemies here at home on the attack. Eventually, the country's resolve gets weaker and weaker. Eventually, after years of fighting a war on two fronts—there and here—we have no choice but to pull out. Eventually, we lose. And don't for a second think Iran is the only country thinking this way—there should be no doubt that Syria, Saudi Arabia and a half-dozen other Muslim countries are doing the same thing also[24].

Unfortunately, this sort of manipulation of the American Left through the use of the American media is in no way limited to Asia or the Middle East. It happens in the Americas as well—South America, more specifically.

On September 18, 2005, Venezuelan President Hugo Chavez began playing the same game—get the media and the Left all riled up against the Bush administration by announcing that we were about to

---

24   There should also be no doubt that there are thousands of Saddam loyalists employing the same strategy—outlined well in advance by Saddam himself—to leverage the hatred of liberals for their own benefit after the military operation itself was done and over with.

invade his country. And why not? It was certainly in his best interest to give Bush another problem. To create more anarchy in the streets. To sow the seeds of dissention before there was even anything to dissent about. To get the ants all fired up. To break the will of the people and to divide and conquer.

Say what you want about Chavez, but he is certainly an incredibly smart guy who knows exactly what he needs to do. And thanks to his country's oil exports, he has all the money he'll ever need to do it. In fact, just four months after getting into the undermine America game, he was able to lure thousands of "activists" from around the world down to Venezuela for a week-long World Social Forum focused mostly on attacking the United States and President Bush.

To get a better feel for exactly what went on down there, we can take a quick look at a couple of excerpts from a January 24, 2006 article about the event—*Venezuela Hosts Anti-US Social Forum*—from Fox News:

> Anne Hess, an activist from Norway, said... "We need the whole world out in the streets again to stop Bush and Blair, and their crazy imperialist dreams."
>
> ...Street vendors sold T-shirts, keychains and watches bearing images of Chavez, Castro and revolutionary hero Che Guevara.

So there it is—thousands of liberals from around the world united together under Chavez to oppose George W. Bush and his "crazy imperialist dreams." Thousands of parasites partying it up in a country run by a dictator intent on undermining the US while he siphons off the wealth of his own country like every other dictator in history has done, acquires weapons from North Korea and other countries hostile to the US and looks to spread communism—with himself as the leader, of course—throughout all of South America. Thousands of liberals in tie-dyed shirts buying Che Guevara watches like they were at a modern-day Grateful Dead concert with Chavez as the 21st century version of Jerry Garcia.

However, although there is no doubt that having all these people come down to Venezuela is certainly a good start, what Chavez really needed to spread the word was a media darling. What Chavez really needed was someone who thinks they are actually doing something useful. What Chavez really needed was an anti-American celebrity. What Chavez really needed was Cindy Sheehan.

Of course, when it comes to favors from the Left, what Chavez wants, Chavez gets and sure enough Sheehan was more than happy to join up with 10,000 other "activists" in Caracas to praise him. A short excerpt from a January 24, 2006 article from AFP News—*US Anti-War Protester Cindy Sheehan Hails Venezuela's Chavez*—gives us even more insight into the situation by telling us that Sheehan said "Venezuela's foreign ministry sponsored her visit."

Venezuela's foreign ministry sponsored her visit. WHAT A SURPRISE! Chavez spends a couple of thousand dollars to fly her down to South America and gets a hundred-million dollars worth of propaganda in return. The deal of the century.

Clearly there are plenty of countries—China, North Korea, Iran, Syria, Venezuela, Cuba and dozens of others hostile to the interests of the United States—that know how to play the game. Unfortunately, these sorts of enemies are not limited only to foreign governments; there are certainly plenty of other kinds of international enemies that we have to deal with—terrorist groups and wealthy individuals being the most dangerous among them.

Take a look at George Soros—a leading advocate and major

financier of the efforts to legalize drug use in the United States. In November, 2003 Soros said that removing George W. Bush from office was the "central focus of my life" and "a matter of life and death." For this purpose, Soros donated $3 million to the Center for American Progress, $5 million to MoveOn.org, and $10 million to America Coming Together[25]—all hyper-liberal organizations which continually make use of all the tools and methodologies discussed throughout this book in order to undermine society and disrupt the social order. One single international Leftist with billions of dollars to spend doing more damage to our country than any military ever could.

And what about Osama bin Laden releasing a tape threatening America just days before the 2004 Presidential election? Clearly, the point of that message was to make people believe that Bush was the root-cause of the Al Qaeda attacks in order to get people to vote for John Kerry. Now I ask you—does bin Laden want the United States to have the strongest possible President in power, or the weakest? The answer is obvious and as usual, the Left is more than happy to oblige.

The Axis of Allies

By now, just about everyone has heard of the Axis of Evil—Iran, Iraq and North Korea. Unfortunately, although each of these countries is certainly a problem in one way or another, they are by no means the only ones the United States needs to concern itself with. No, that extended list would also have to include the likes of Venezuela, Cuba, Syria and

---

25   Overall, according to the Center for Responsive Politics, Soros donated more than $23 million to various 527 Groups dedicated to defeating President George Bush, all while doing everything he could to try to ban "soft money" contributions to federal election campaigns.

at least a dozen others that are actively hostile to us, not to mention terrorist organizations like Al Qaeda, Hezbollah and so forth. So with all these different groups hating us, we should at least be glad that we have some friends to count on—or do we?

Unfortunately, although many countries purport to be our allies, they always seem to do everything they possibly could to undermine us. No, they are not openly hostile to the United States, but they do regularly employ all sorts of tactics—mostly in the form of passive aggressiveness and some very clever manipulation of the Left—to hurt us in every way they can. Sure they may claim to be our allies, but when push comes to shove, their true agenda comes through loud and clear. It is for this reason that I call these countries the *Axis of Allies*.

And just who are the Axis of Allies? Well, some of the most visible members of the group would have to included France, Germany, Canada, Mexico, Turkey and Saudi Arabia. These are just a few of the countries that have no qualms about coming to us when they need something, then turning around and spiting on us when they don't.

France, of course, has long history of undermining the United States going back to at least the early twentieth century when Prime Minister George Clemenceau announced with typical French arrogance that "America is the only nation in history which miraculously has gone directly from barbarism to degeneration without the usual interval of civilization."

But more recently, France has done things like refuse to arrest the Lebanese Hezbollah leader who masterminded the plot that killed 241 Marines in Beirut as he strolled through Paris back in 1985; refuse to allow the US to fly F-111's from the UK over its airspace to destroy Libyan terrorist camps after they bombed a crowded Berlin nightclub killing American soldiers; continued doing billions of dollars of business with Saddam Hussein after UN sanctions were put in place in the early nineties and, of course, did everything possible to prevent the US from taking out Hussein despite his violation of nearly twenty different UN resolutions.

The same is true of Germany. They too did everything they could under the guise of "peace" to obstruct the US when it came to dealing with Iraq. However, once the military action was completed and we started looking a little deeper into the situation, it was clear that they were also involved in all sorts of secret arrangements with Saddam. Not surprisingly they—like France—were also owed billions of dollars from past business dealings and had a huge vested interest in keeping Saddam in power to protect this investment.

Then we have Turkey which, as a member of NATO, was more than happy to have the US protect them from the Soviet Union and other threats. Yet the one time we needed them, they pulled the rug out from under us at the last minute by refusing to allow the 4th Infantry Division to advance into northern Iraq from their soil after all the equipment was already in place to do so.

The same was true of both Kuwait and Saudi Arabia. Neither allowed the US to launch an attack into Iraq or even set up an operations control center in their countries despite the fact that they were more than happy to have us around when Saddam Hussein was terrorizing them only ten years earlier.

Of course, Canada—our neighbor to the north—is a well known repository of Anti-Americanism, just as Mexico—our neighbor to the South—is more than happy to undermine us culturally and economically as it continues to refuse to make any attempt to curtail illegal immigration into the US.

Just as all these countries are more than happy to act in ways that are exactly the opposite of what one would expect from a friend or an ally, they all seem to know just how to leverage the Left to fuel the fires of hatred inside this country and make it that much harder to get anything done. After all, how can we ever do anything if *France hates us?* If *Germany hates us?* If *everybody hates us?*

So who are our real allies? In terms of major players, pretty much only Great Britain, Israel and Australia as far as I can tell—although liberals in those countries are certainly doing everything they can to change that. After all, the headline in the Daily Mirror—one of Britain's largest newspapers—on the day after George Bush won re-election was simply: *How can 59,054,087 people be so DUMB?*

Sure sounds like liberalism to me.

Conclusions

Since the end of the Vietnam War, several key members of the North Vietnamese military have openly admitted that the only thing that kept them going in the face of certain defeat was the anarchy caused by the anti-war mafia back in the US. In fact, in an interview with the Wall Street Journal a couple of years ago, North Vietnamese Colonel Bui Tin credited the anti-war movement with being "essential to our strategy," and said visits to Hanoi by people like former Attorney General Ramsey Clark[26] and Jane Fonda "gave us confidence that we should hold on in the face of battlefield reverses." He summed up the situation very nicely by saying that "Through dissent and protest [the United States] lost the ability to mobilize a will to win."

---

26   Clark—a staunch supporter of John Kerry in the 2004 Presidential race—is affiliated with VoteToImpeach.org, an organization advocating the impeachment of George Bush, has been an opponent of both Gulf wars, is the founder of the International Action Center, an affiliate of the Workers' World Party and a co-founder of ANSWER (Act Now to Stop War and End Racism). He is also one of the lawyers defending Saddam Hussein in his trial in Iraq.

Unfortunately, things are no different today than they were thirty of forty years ago. Liberals are still aligned with America's enemies and are still doing everything they possibly can to destroy our national unity and undermine our will to win.

The Clintons were—and still are—very cozy with the communist Chinese. As a result, they've gotten millions of dollars in illegal campaign contributions and gained tremendous political power; in return, the Chinese have gotten the advanced guidance technology they needed for their long-range nuclear missiles.

As Secretary of State, Madeleine Albright was so easily manipulated by the ego-stroking charade Kim Jong-il put on for her honor during her visit to North Korea that she happily looked the other way while the country continued on with its nuclear program.

Jesse Jackson and Harry Belafonte have begun partying it up in Venezuela with Hugo Chavez as they discuss the evils of American democracy. Ace reporter Sean Penn now spends time over to Iran trying to give credibility to a despotic government and undermine the Bush Administration's attempts to reign in that country's nuclear program.

Time after time we see liberals working with groups hostile to the interests of the United States. Time after time we see money coming in from organizations like International Answer and the Worker's World Party to finance the events—"peace" protests, "civil-rights" rallies, anti-capitalism marches and so on—of the American Left. Time after time we see how simple it is for foreign governments or some sort of front group hostile to the interests of the US to throw a few dollars at a bunch of filthy liberals and let the degenerates who have already leached off our society their entire lives do the rest.

The whole situation is a win-win relationship—at least for them. For liberals, they are given an endless source of propaganda to use however they want to undermine the very government that has given them everything. They get their causes financed—special rights, exemptions from responsibility, affirmative action, diversity, gun control, a weakened military, gay-marriage, higher taxes, lower productivity, wealth distribution rather than wealth creation and anything else that gives them something for nothing and destroys whatever semblance of a meritocracy we still have left in this country.

In return, these foreign governments get exactly what they want—a confused, weakened and disoriented America, along with carte blanch to do whatever they want regardless of the eventual consequences to us. Want to develop nuclear weapons? Sure, no problem. Want to attack Taiwan? Sure, no problem. Want to take over the oilfields in the Mideast and South America and have the US economy grind to a halt? Sure—be our guests. After all, we're liberals. After all, we're open-minded. After all, we want to give peace a chance. After all, we hate the same exact people you do.

Since foreign governments have no way to beat us militarily and cannot beat us economically, they have only one other option at their disposal. That option is destroy us from within. That option is to use our own freedoms against us. That option is create, encourage and exploit every possible form of propaganda they possibly can to make the American people think and act in ways that are contrary to the best interests of this country. That option is to partner up with liberals and let them do the rest.

Furthermore, it should be immediately clear that the US could—with regard to each and every situation or policy decision it ever faces—determine the best course of action for itself by simply thinking through what so many of these hostile foreign governments want for us and then doing the exact opposite.

Would China want us to actually build a wall on the border with Mexico and then deport all the illegal aliens who are already here? Does

Iran want the whole issue of gay-marriage in the US to just go away? Is there any chance at all that North Korea would ever want the US to stop affirmative action? In each of these cases, the answer is exactly the same—of course not. These countries know that each of these things— and so many other liberal programs and ideas—divides and weakens us as a nation, so they want nothing more than to see them continue.

If nothing else, this simple litmus test should tell us exactly what to do—and what not to do—in each and every situation we face. And guess which side of the equation liberals will always be on—the wrong side. The same side as all the hostile foreign governments who are doing everything they can to undermine our society.

THIRTEEN

A Swarm of Ants

How is it that so many hard-working, intelligent and more-often-than-not, honest, objective and unbiased people living in the United States of America are actually afraid to say what they really think?

How is it that homosexuals—who barely make up 1-2% of the population—are the focus of so much news, so much attention and so much endless glorification in movies, magazines, books and television shows?

How is it that the most absolute, clear-cut and undeniable discrimination that exists within our society is not just tolerated, but fanatically encouraged as long as it is done under the guise of diversity?

How is it that the people who are so consumed by their own hatred that they can't even see straight are the ones who are always claiming—and almost always granted—the moral high-ground when it comes to things like prejudice, tolerance, human rights, war, peace, justice and equality?

How could the world we live in possibly be so upside down? How can any civilized society allow these things to go on? How can these kinds of absurdities continue to dominate our lives more and more each day? And the most important question of all—how come no one seems to be able to stop it?

Well, the first thing we need to do in order to see why all these things are happening is to step back and look at the dynamics of human behavior. Once we do, it becomes immediately clear that the answer to all these questions ultimately come down to one simple thing—an ancient Japanese proverb that tells us: *The fiercest serpent may be overcome by a swarm of ants.*

It was this simple concept that allowed Admiral Yamamoto to destroy the American Fleet at Pearl Harbor. It was this simple reality which drove the US out of Vietnam. It continues to be this simple idea that has given generations of terrorists—or anyone engaged in any sort of asymmetrical warfare—the ability to strike fear into adversaries thousands of times more powerful than they are. And it happens to be this same simple dynamic that has allowed liberalism to lead us to where we are today.

The fiercest serpent may be overcome by a swarm of ants. In nature, bacteria use this same principle. In nature, viruses use the same principle. We know that one bacterium by itself is harmless. We know that one virus alone means nothing. But when millions upon millions of them work together to infect a host, they can cause anything from a cold, to a flu, to an infection to a slow and painful death simply by overwhelming every part of the body until it can no longer function. Ants, bees, locusts and wasps all use the same strategy—overwhelm, overwhelm, overwhelm.

In the same way, by simply watching the Left operate, we can immediately see that all the destructive power of liberalism is the result of this singular dynamic. Like bacteria, one liberal by itself is powerless—but they never work by themselves, do they? No, they work in unison. They work in packs. They work in swarms. Millions and millions of them screaming, protesting, chanting, blogging, boycotting, harassing, suing, extorting, undermining, criticizing and labeling over and over and over again.

This is exactly the sort of thing that rational people have to deal with every day of their lives. Conservative politicians, the military, the police, anyone trying to do something constructive—swarm after swarm from every direction attacking you personally, socially, politically and financially, with names, intimidation, slander and endless threats to your livelihood.

They come out of the television—channel after channel, show after show, anchor after anchor, speech after speech. They riot in the streets. They infest the House, the Senate, the courts and the schools. They live in the newspapers—journalists, clawing and scratching after any story, any statement, any event and any tragedy they could exploit to make people look bad.

Ant after ant doing everything they could possibly get away with, all the while constantly changing the laws so they can always get away with more. So you can't even defend yourself. So you are guilty until proven innocent. Until the swarms of hatred, defiance, communism and atheism have completely and totally destroyed the evil serpent known as America.

The Art of the Swarm

We all know how a swarm works. Someone or something wanders into place they should not have gone and inadvertently agitates a few members of an insect colony. As soon as this happens, they immediately send a frantic signal out to the others—attack! Suddenly, thousands of ants, bees, hornets or wasps stop whatever they may be doing and immediately oblige in the assault of the intruder.

Not surprisingly, liberal swarms are no different. In fact, liberal swarms protect their territory in exactly the same way insects do except liberal swarms are a thousand times more vicious.

Liberal swarms will systematically attack and destroy anything that could ever be a threat to them. Anything that might get people to think. Anything that might get people to take responsibility for themselves. Anything that could ever possibly threaten the liberal hornet's nest of special rights, preferential treatment, defiance and victimization.

Liberal swarms will relentlessly attack any sort of program meant to get people do something productive. They will attack anything that might require them to contribute something to society. Anything that might hint at any sort of maturity. Anything that would actually prevent them from doing whatever they want, whenever they want, to whoever they want without any regard whatsoever for anyone other than themselves.

Just try to have a meaningful discussion on anything—anything at all—when liberals are around. Try talking honestly about race. Try to criticize something a black, Hispanic, Asian or Muslim may have done. Just try to hold them up to the same standards as the root of all evil— the white male. Just try it. Try it once and see what you get: *Racist!*

Then try it again, this time clarifying your point to make sure everyone knows that you're addressing the person's behavior, not their race. Now what do you get?

Racist! Racist! Racist! Racist! Racist! Racist! Racist! Racist! Racist! Racist! Racist! Racist!

By this point most people will have already given up and run for their lives. But what if you challenge the ants? What if you try to get them to actually address the issue? Big mistake. Big, big, *big* mistake because now you are not just dealing with one or two liberals; now you're dealing with all of them.

Suddenly, they appear from nowhere. Neighbors, co-workers, pedestrians and people you have never even seen before waving around cameras, microphones, bullhorns and signs: *Racist! Racist!*

Ant after ant. Millions of screamers, thousands of bloggers, hundreds of journalists, dozens of networks. Day and night. Day and night. Day and night. *Racist! Racist! Racist! Racist! Racist! Racist! Racist! Racist! Racist! Racist! Racist!*

Of course, I'm not saying everything is like that. For example, say you happened to the President of Harvard and wanted to understand some of the differences between men and women (not that there are any, of course—except that women are better), then what do you get? Well, this time the ants take another form:

Sexist! Misogynist! Male Chauvinist Pig! Pig! Pig! We hate you, pig! Oink! Oink! Oink! Oink! Sexist! Sexist! Sexist! Sexist! Sexist! We hate you, pig! We hate you, pig! Sexist! Sexist! Sexist! Sexist! Sexist! We hate you, pig! Oink! Oink! Oink! Sexist! Sexist! Sexist! Sexist! Sexist! Sexist! Sexist! Sexist! Sexist! Sexist! Misogynist! Misogynist! Misogynist! Misogynist! Sexist! Misogynist! Sexist! Sexist! Sexist! Oink! Oink! Oink! Oink!

Now ask yourself—are you opposed to gay marriage? Do you think the whole thing may be a farce? Do you think it might not be a good idea for one reason or another? Well if you do, I have some advice for you—don't bother to try to have a discussion about it. Don't dare mention your opinion to anyone. Don't even dare to think about it.

Give in. Give them their way. Surrender. Back off. Go into the basement and cower behind the furnace because if you don't, the ants are coming for you:

HOMOPHOBE! HOMOPHOBE!

Now if you happen to be just an ordinary citizen, you should consider yourself lucky because in that case, you might only have to deal with a few ants. But for a public figure, it could easily be hundreds, thousand or even millions of ants. Millions of parasites crawling all over you for days, weeks, months and sometimes years until you have no choice but to give in.

Go watch the Gay Pride parade sometime. This is what you can expect to hear as the ants march down the street, destroying everything in their path: *I'm here, I'm queer, I'll be here next year! I'm here, I'm queer, I'll be here next year! I'm here, I'm queer, I'll be here next year! I'm here, I'm queer, I'll be here next year! I'm here, I'm queer, I'll be here next year! I'm here, I'm queer, I'll be here next year! I'm here, I'm queer, I'll be here next year! I'm here, I'm queer, I'll be here next year! I'm here, I'm queer, I'll be here next year!*

Ant after ant. Chant after chant. Screaming, whistles, bullhorns, water balloons and half-naked men simulating all sorts of sex acts in the middle of the street. Who could put up with that? No one. So you don't put up with it. You leave town. You move. You stop arguing. You let them have special rights, hoping they'll stop. But they never do and they never will.

Anyone remember Rodney King? Anyone care about the police? Anyone care about the circumstances? Anyone care about the network coverage specifically designed to drive people into a frenzy? Anyone care about the billions of dollars of damage or about the endless looting that was all done under the guise of equality?

Well if you do, the liberal ants are ready to crawl all over you: *No Justice, no peace! No Justice, no peace! No Justice, no peace! No Justice, no peace! No Justice, no peace! No Justice, no peace! No Justice, no peace! No Justice, no peace! No Justice, no peace! No Justice, no peace! No Justice, no peace! No Justice, no peace! No Justice, no peace! No Justice, no peace! No Justice, no peace! No Justice, no peace! No Justice, no peace! No Justice, no peace! No Justice, no peace! No Justice, no peace!*

Need more proof of the liberal swarms infesting our society? Just read any paper, watch CNN, go to any liberal website or better yet, just do a search on Google. Search terms like *Bush, hatred, racist, sexist, homophobe, bigot* or *war*. Search any of these words and you'll immediately see thousands and thousands of websites attacking anything with any constructive purpose instantly appear before your eyes. Millions of ants you never even knew existed, all working behind the scenes twenty-four hours a day to undermine and corrupt the society you worked so hard to build and protect. Millions and millions and millions of them, all revved up and ready to go. Just dare to give them a reason.

Ants in Action

So just how are these liberal swarms destroying America? How about their effect on the military, for one?

Thanks to all the America-haters running Hollywood these days, television and movies are constantly ridiculing and vilifying the military. Thanks to the ants in academia, colleges around the country are banning military recruiters. Thanks to the news media, any situation that could ever make the military look bad—like Tailhook or Abu Gharib—is presented over and over again in most negative ways possible for years on end.

War protestors. Lawyers in the DOD. Embedded journalists just waiting for that one mistake so they can find another Marine to crucify. Parasites spitting in the faces of soldiers. Condemnations by the UN. Endless criticism by foreign governments. Snide comments from liberal politicians here at home. Swarm after swarm attacking, undermining, sabotaging and destroying.

As a result of these withering attacks, military recruitment is down. As a result of these withering attacks, the military is becoming overly cautious in everything it does. As a result of these withering attacks, more American soldiers are being killed every day in Iraq. As a result of these withering attacks, the American military—the fiercest serpent the world has ever known—is slowly being brought to their knees by nothing more than a swarm of ants.

Now take a look at another area where the ants are hard at work—reparations. According to a July 20, 2005 article written by the well known conservative columnist, Walter E. Williams, "The slavery reparations shakedown lobby... failed in the courts and Congress, so they're going after weak-kneed CEOs." Williams also goes on to write:

CEOs at J.P. Morgan Chase Bank and Wachovia Corp. have...agreed to be shaken down for several million dollars... What are we to make of corporate CEOs, and their boards of directors, who cave in to the reparations shakedown? What are their motivations?

Clearly, their motivations are to avoid endless boycotts and continued harassment by the NAACP and the likes of Typhoid Jesse, Al Sharpton and the other race-baiters. Clearly their motivations are to avoid the billions of dollars they may ultimately be forced to pay out through frivolous lawsuits brought by liberal attorneys looking for a quick payday. Clearly their motivations are to avoid all the bad publicity that the liberal media will pile up on them until they finally capitulate. Clearly their motivations are to avoid the swarm of ants.

So what other things have the ants done? How about pushing more class-action lawsuits which, in the instant a verdict is announced, can destroy what it took a man a lifetime to build. Guns, tobacco, fast food and pharmaceuticals. You name it, if there is money to be made, opportunities to be exploited or success to be undermined, you can bet your life the ants will be there.

Want more examples? Just think about the situations where conservatives have tried to speak on college campuses. What do people like Ann Coulter, Sean Hannity, David Horowitz, Daniel Flynn and others have to deal with just for trying to tell people they should be responsible for their own actions? You know the answer. You've read about it, seen the footage or at least heard about it on the radio. What they have to deal with is people screaming at the tops of their lungs, tearing up flyers, heckling them, throwing pies in their faces and doing everything they can to undermine free speech and stop conservatives from even having a chance say something without the media spinning it into some form of hate crime.

Conclusions

I was wondering if it would be possible for a liberal to explain their position on an issue without making personal attacks against other people.

Ant.

Every time I try to have a rational discussion with them, all they ever do is throw a tirade.

Ant. Ant. Ant. Ant. Ant. Ant.

I would think that if they really cared about an issue, that they would try, just once...

Ant. Ant. Ant. Ant. Ant. Ant. Ant. Ant. Ant. Ant. Ant. Ant. Ant. Ant.

Let me start again—that they would try, just once, to structure an argument that didn't involve... attacking other...

Ant. Ant. Ant. Ant. Ant. Ant. Ant. Ant. Ant. Ant. Ant. Ant. Ant. Ant. Ant. Ant. Ant. Ant. Ant. Ant. Ant. Ant. Ant. Ant. Ant. Ant. Ant. Ant. Ant. Ant. Ant. Ant. Ant. Ant. Ant. Ant. Ant. Ant. Ant. Ant. Ant. Ant.

God, what is going on? What are these things?

Ant. Ant. Ant. Ant. Ant. Ant. Ant. Ant. Ant. Ant. Ant. Ant. Ant. Ant. Ant. Ant. Ant. Ant. Ant. Ant. Ant. Ant. Ant. Ant. Ant. Ant. Ant. Ant. Ant. Ant. Ant. Ant. Ant. Ant. Ant. Ant. Ant. Ant. Ant. Ant. Ant. Ant. Ant. Ant. Ant. Ant. Ant. Ant. Ant. Ant. Ant. Ant. Ant. Ant. Ant. Ant. Ant. Ant. Ant. Ant. Ant. Ant. Ant. Ant. Ant. Ant. Ant. Ant. Ant. Ant. Ant. Ant. Ant. Ant. Ant. Ant. Ant. Ant. Ant. Ant. Ant. Ant. Ant.

What do you people want? Why do you insist on putting words in my mouth? Why are you calling me all those names? Why do you follow me everywhere I go? Get that microphone out of my face. Stay away. What are you screaming about?

Ant. Ant.

What the...? How do I get these things off of me!

Ant. Ant.

Alright—The United States is the worst country in history! Our solders are baby killers! Reagan was an idiot!

Ant. Ant. Ant. Ant. Ant. Ant. Ant. Ant. Ant. Ant. Ant. Ant. Ant. Ant. Ant. Ant. Ant. Ant. Ant. Ant. Ant. Ant. Ant. Ant. Ant. Ant. Ant. Ant. Ant. Ant. Ant. Ant. Ant. Ant. Ant. Ant. Ant. Ant. Ant. Ant. Ant. Ant. Ant. Ant. Ant. Ant. Ant. Ant. Ant. Ant. Ant. Ant. Ant. Ant. Ant. Ant. Ant. Ant. Ant. Ant. Ant. Ant. Ant. Ant. Ant. Ant. Ant. Ant. Ant. Ant. Ant. Ant. Ant. Ant. Ant. Ant. Ant. Ant. Ant. Ant. Ant. Ant. Ant. Ant. Ant. Ant. Ant. Ant.

Yes, you're right—women are better than men. All police are racist. Illegal immigrants should be given millions of dollars each. Per person. Per child. *Per word of English they've ever been forced to speak!*

Ant. Ant. Ant. Ant. Ant. Ant. Ant. Ant. Ant. Ant. Ant. Ant. Ant. Ant. Ant. Ant. Ant. Ant. Ant. Ant. Ant. Ant. Ant. Ant. Ant. Ant. Ant. Ant. Ant. Ant. Ant. Ant. Ant. Ant. Ant. Ant. Ant. Ant. Ant. Ant. Ant. Ant. Ant. Ant. Ant. Ant. Ant. Ant. Ant. Ant. Ant. Ant. Ant. Ant. Ant. Ant. Ant. Ant. Ant. Ant. Ant. Ant. Ant. Ant. Ant. Ant. Ant. Ant. Ant. Ant. Ant. Ant. Ant. Ant. Ant. Ant. Ant. Ant. Ant. Ant. Ant. Ant. Ant. Ant. Ant.

Yes, we've sinned against you! We used merit in our hiring practices, not diversity. We tried to look at things logically, not superficially. We've tried to solve problems while they were still manageable and to teach people to do things for themselves. I admit it. I'm sorry, okay; just please go away!

Ant. Ant. Ant. Ant. Ant. Ant. Ant. Ant. Ant. Ant. Ant. Ant. Ant. Ant. Ant. Ant. Ant. Ant. Ant. Ant. Ant. Ant. Ant. Ant. Ant. Ant. Ant. Ant. Ant. Ant. Ant. Ant. Ant. Ant. Ant. Ant. Ant. Ant. Ant. Ant. Ant. Ant. Ant. Ant. Ant. Ant. Ant. Ant. Ant. Ant. Ant. Ant. Ant. Ant. Ant. Ant. Ant. Ant. Ant. Ant. Ant. Ant. Ant. Ant. Ant. Ant. Ant. Ant. Ant. Ant. Ant. Ant. Ant. Ant. Ant. Ant. Ant. Ant. Ant. Ant. Ant. Ant.

I apologize. I apologize. Please, just let me go on with my life!

Ant. Ant. Ant. Ant. Ant. Ant. Ant. Ant. Ant. Ant. Ant. Ant. Ant. Ant. Ant. Ant. Ant. Ant. Ant. Ant. Ant. Ant. Ant. Ant. Ant. Ant. Ant. Ant. Ant. Ant. Ant. Ant. Ant. Ant. Ant. Ant. Ant. Ant. Ant. Ant. Ant. Ant. Ant. Ant. Ant. Ant. Ant. Ant. Ant. Ant. Ant. Ant. Ant. Ant. Ant. Ant. Ant. Ant. Ant. Ant. Ant. Ant. Ant. Ant. Ant. Ant. Ant. Ant. Ant. Ant. Ant. Ant.

We'll give you anything you want—just leave us alone! Name your price!

Ant. Ant. Ant. Ant. Ant. Ant. Ant. Ant. Ant. Ant. Ant. Ant. Ant. Ant. Ant. Ant. Ant. Ant. Ant. Ant. Ant. Ant. Ant. Ant. Ant. Ant. Ant. Ant. Ant. Ant. Ant. Ant. Ant. Ant.

Name your price!

Suddenly, a cease fire. The Queen has spoken. Hillary or Boxer. Sarandon or Streisand. Sheehan or Fonda. Schumer or Kennedy or Jesse or Sharpton. The ants have heard the magic words. The ants have achieved victory. The ants have brought down the serpent of logic, capitalism, meritocracy and justice.

The ants have swarmed all over you until there was nothing left. Until a man didn't have any fight left in him. Until a company was on the verge of bankruptcy. Until the military was gutted, the police emasculated, the borders broken and the country overrun by terrorists and perverts.

The ants have stopped their attack—but they don't just leave. They take something with them. All of them. They take a piece of you back to nest. They take more than they could have ever earned. They take more than they could ever need. They take what you built, what you made, what you struggled for and what you deserve. They take it and leave you with nothing. They take money, jobs, liberty and rights. They take roles in academia. They take positions in government. They take seats on the Boards of companies whose businesses they couldn't even begin to understand.

They take your product. They take your service. They take your dignity and reputation. They take everything they possibly can and leave absolutely nothing behind that isn't nailed to the floor.

And you've been warned. *Don't do it again! Don't say it again! Don't even think it again!* Remember what we ants can do. Remember we'll be watching. Remember we'll be listening. Remember there are millions of us ready to come back on a moment's notice. Just give us a reason. An

165

excuse. A guise. Give us something to do other than to earn our own way, other than to allow freedom of speech, of thought, of opportunity or of religion. Other than to let you defend yourself, your home, your country or your opinion. Remember to do what we say or we'll back. Remember what it felt like to have us crawling all over you.

Remember you racist, capitalist, American pig. *Remember.*

FOURTEEN

Guises

One of the best ways for liberals to deflect criticism or justify getting something for nothing is to hide behind some sort of guise. Disguise their attack against one group as an effort to help another. Disguise their hatred as outrage. Disguise their failure as oppression. Disguise their real agenda in any way they possibly can in order to make the maliciousness of it seem as though it was actually meant to be benign.

This strategy of obscuring motivations has always been an incredibly powerful tool for liberals. For one, it immediately makes their actions, their behaviors and their purported ideology exceedingly difficult to argue with—at least superficially. Second, it often tends to exploit those elements of society who actually need some sort of help, ultimately using them as pawns to force the hands of others. Third—and maybe most importantly—it provides the most convenient way possible for liberals to avoid the real issue.

Not that this sort of behavior is anything new, mind you. Going back thousands of years, we recall that even the Bible spoke about how evil will always disguise itself as good. And why not—what better way could there possibly be for someone to get what they want than to surreptitiously exploit the compassion, the sympathies and the inherent desire of others to try to do the right thing?

So just what are the guises that liberals hide behind? Unfortunately, there are just too many of them to keep track of. That being said, it could still be useful for us to take a look at some of the more popular ones:

Racism

Probably the single most pervasive guise in United States of America today is that of racism. Does racism exist? Of course it does—but not nearly to the extent liberals would like us to believe. After all, how many times have you or someone you know been called a *racist* for something that had absolutely nothing to do with race? Five times? Fifty times? Fifty-thousand times?

Not that the actual number matters, really. The point is that for almost all of us, the answer to this question would be best summarized by three simple words—*virtually every time*. Virtually every time liberals have called you or someone you know a racist, the issue at hand had absolutely nothing whatsoever to do with judging someone based on race.

Now take this same situation and multiply it by millions and millions of liberals making million and millions of accusations about racism and you end up with the conclusion that virtually every time you hear the word racist—whether it be on the news, in a debate, in a congressional hearing or anywhere else—that the allegation has absolutely no merit whatsoever.

By the way—why is it that liberals always want us to believe that racism is only limited to white people? I've certainly met plenty of blacks, Asians, Hispanics and Muslims but who were absolute, obsessive, ranting, vile racists down to the core—but somehow, they always seem to get away with it. Why? Because racism is a guise—a guise to get anything the people using it ever want.

At this point, most people who have seen the Left in action should know that the term *racist* is so overused that it has for all practical purposes, become absolutely meaningless—at least in terms of the idea it was originally meant to convey.

That being the case, we should feel morally obligated to establish a new definition for the word based solely on the context in which it tends to be used. As such, we can now define the term *racist* to mean: i) *any person willing to have an honest discussion on race; or ii) one who holds all people to the same moral, ethical and intellectual standards regardless of their race or religion.*

Feminism

This section could have just as easily been called *Sexism*, but feminism is essentially the same guise, only a little broader and a lot more vicious.

Liberal women love to hide behind the guise of feminism whenever they can. Want to make more money without having to do anything to earn it? Simply invoke feminism. Want to justify your hostility towards men on college campuses? Simply invoke feminism. Want to brainwash young boys with all sorts of anti-male propaganda? Simply say the magic word: feminism.

Sexism, feminism, misogyny—all different ways of saying the same meaningless thing. All words liberal women can always count on to justify their endless attacks on men. All words they can use to get something for nothing. All words they can use to rationalize their demands for absolute exemption from any sort of responsibility, accountability or criticism. All words they can use whenever they have no possible way to win a debate on any sort of gender-related issue.

As with racism, most people who have seen the Left in action should know that the term *sexist* is so overused that it has also become absolutely meaningless. That being the case, we should once again feel morally obligated to establish a new definition for the word based solely on its popular context.

As such, we can now redefine a sexist to be: *i) any person willing to have an honest discussion on the differences between men and women; in particular, one who actually wants to understand the basis for such differences; and ii) any person who holds all people to the same moral, ethical and intellectual standards regardless of their gender.*

Homophobia

Not surprisingly, homophobia is essentially the same guise as racism and sexism, except in this case, instead of being a guise used for the benefit of women and minorities, it is a guise that is actually used for the benefit of white males. Gay white males, of course.

As with both racism and sexism, most people know the term *homophobe* is so overused that it too has become absolutely meaningless. That being the case, we again feel obligated to establish a new definition for the word based solely on the way it is generally used by the Left.

As such, from this point onward, the definition of a homophobe shall be: *i) any person not willing to grant special rights or preferences to homosexuals; and ii) any person who holds all people to the same moral, ethical and intellectual standards regardless of their sexual orientation.*

Hate Crimes

Hate crimes fall into the category of what I call a *guise of guises* since they are nothing more than another guise to further extract value from the three guises—racism, sexism and homophobia—which we just discussed.

Liberals are always talking about things like freedom, rights, justice and equality. Yet, not surprisingly, liberals seem to have evolved the unusual idea that certain people are in fact, more equal than others. Given this distorted belief system, it should come as no surprise that they do everything possible to give these very special people very special rights, privileges, immunities and protections—all through the guise known as hate crimes.

Dissent

The dictionary definition of dissent is generally something along the lines of "to differ in opinion or feeling; to disagree"—and it is exactly this sort of definition that liberals hide behind when invoking this particular guise.

Unfortunately for the Left, making all sorts of personal attacks on people is not what any rational society would ever consider to be dissent. Instead, dissent would be saying something along the lines of "We shouldn't go to war in Iraq because we need to focus on countries we know are actively supporting terrorism; going after Iraq would be exactly the sort of distraction we can't afford."

But how often do we ever hear this sort of legitimate dissent from liberals?—Maybe five percent of the time. Maybe. And what do we hear the other ninety-five percent? You guessed it: *Racist! Nazi! War-monger! Stupid religious rightwing Jesus-freak asshole! Stealing oil! No blood for oil! Not in my name! Neo-conservative Hitler! Imperialist child-killer!* Do any of these sorts of things have anything whatsoever to do with dissent? Not even close.

Also, since we happen to be on the subject, I should point out that the guise of dissent also operates under several other names—peace protestors, activism, freedom of speech and environmental rights just to name a few. But no matter what name it hides behind, dissent is clearly nothing more than just another guise for liberals to attack conservatives. Nothing more than just another guise for anarchists to wreak havoc. Nothing more than just another guise to get together, bang drums, blow whistles, smoke pot and scream out whatever garbage pops into their feeble little minds. Nothing more than just another guise to help liberals undermine our society.

Diversity

Liberals love diversity—as long it can be used as a euphemism for "no heterosexual white males allowed." But what about things like about diversity of opinion on college campuses? Don't even think about it.

By the way, if you happen to be black and conservative—or a woman and a conservative—liberals will immediately revoke your diversity visa. Why? Because diversity is nothing more than a guise. Diversity is nothing more than a scam. Diversity is what you focus on when quality just doesn't matter.

Make no mistake about it; liberals love the guise of diversity—the inclusion of certain people through the exclusion of others. But in reality, diversity is nothing more than a nicer way of saying divisiveness—

the favorite tool of the liberal.

Compassion, Tolerance and Sensitivity

The collective guises of compassion, tolerance and sensitivity are nothing less than the Trojan horse through which all other liberal guises operate. Under the cover of these three honorable concepts—in perhaps the greatest scam ever devised—liberals are slowly, systematically and relentless destroying the freedoms, values, strengths and opportunities of our society.

But how can compassion, sensitivity and tolerance possibly be so destructive? Simple — these words have nothing whatsoever to do with the situations they are applied to and there is never any sort of reciprocity provided by the groups which benefit the most from them.

Whereas conservatives are expected—often forced—to give liberals anything they want under the guise of these concepts, liberals have absolutely no compassion for conservatives, have absolutely no tolerance for conservative ideas and have absolutely no sensitivity when it comes to how anything they do or say may affect anyone but them.

Essentially, the guises of compassion, tolerance and sensitivity ultimately mean "let liberals do whatever they want, say whatever they want, attack you however they want and be as irresponsible as they want"—all while you sit there like an idiot and pay for it all.

Civil Rights

The notion of civil rights is regularly abused by liberals in exactly the same ways as every other guise — to get what they want without having to work for it and to do everything possible to undermine authority.

Forget the whole concept of civil rights as it was understood in the sixties. These days—regardless of what liberals may claim—everyone already has all the rights they could ever possibly need. But regardless of this, liberals must have something to complain about; after all, why let a perfectly good guise go to waste? So what issues do the liberals of today apply this guise to? Why those things having to do with any sort of responsibility of course.

These days, having to go through a metal detector before getting on an airplane is a violation of a person's civil rights. These days, expecting someone from another country to not come here illegally is a violation of their civil rights. These days, not being allowed to spit into the face of a police officer is violation of civil rights. These days, anything not covered by some other guise can always be said to be a violation of liberal civil rights.

Human Rights

Want an example of the sort of things this guise focuses on? All we need to do is to take a look at a couple of excerpts from an October, 2003 report put out by Human Rights Watch (www.hrw.org)—the largest "human rights" group in the country:

> "... U.S. soldiers can be arrogant and abusive. They have been seen putting their feet on detained Iraqis' heads —— a highly insulting offense..."
>
> "Human Rights Watch strongly recommended that U.S. forces desist from the practice of putting their feet on the heads of Iraqis whom they have detained...

In Iraqi culture, the use of feet against another person is highly insulting and offensive."

You know life in this country has become way too easy when there are entire organizations that have nothing better to do than worry about the possibility of someone being insulted in the middle of a war.

Education

Make no mistake about it—by education, liberals really mean re-education. Rarely, if ever, do you hear liberals talk about things like reading, writing, math, logic, analytical thinking or problem solving. Instead, they focus on general statements about needing more money for education while supporting ways to have more and more of it spent on garbage like gay studies, women's studies, African-American studies, Asian-American studies, Native-American studies and any other form of anti-American divisiveness they could possibly get away with.

But these are just the tip of the iceberg. These are just what liberals want to teach in elementary school, middle-school, high-school and college. What about all the people who have already gone through school; what can liberals do about that?

They could always find new ways to educate them, of course. How about requiring all companies to provide sexual harassment training at work? How about transgender sensitivity classes for San Francisco police officers? How about mandatory "Homophobia in the Workplace" workshops like the ones Motorola requires for its employees? How about liberals doing everything they possibly can to indoctrinate people under the guise of education?

By the way, take a look at the people who are always calling for "educating" us about one thing or another. I don't know about you, but I've always found it incredibly interesting how the least intelligent members of society are always the ones who want to do the most educating.

Offended

I have to admit that my favorite liberal guise of them all is the claim of being offended. Tell a child to clean her room—chances she'll be offended. Tell a child to eat his vegetables—chances are he'll be offended. Tell your children to shut off the television and do their math homework—chances are they'll be offended.

Like children, liberals are always offended by anything they don't want to hear. Liberals are always offended by anything that doesn't directly cater to them. Liberals are always offended by anything that might make them look at a situation objectively. Liberals are always offended by anything that might require them to actually act like an adult.

FIFTEEN

Other Methods

Over the course of this book, we have explored several of the primary tools and methodologies used by liberals in their never-ending quest to undermine society and disrupt the social order. Unfortunately, liberals have developed so many ways to distort reality that our list will always remain far from complete.

That being said, I felt it was important to at least touch on a few of the lesser techniques and behaviors liberals use to achieve these goals in the hope that these secondary strategies will become just as obvious to anyone interested in understanding them as the ones we have already discussed.

Controlling the Media

No matter how much propaganda the Left may put out on this issue, there is no doubt whatsoever that liberals control the media. Pick up just about any major newspaper and what do you see—attacks against conservatives and praise for liberals. Criticism after criticism of everything conservatives do. Harping on any sort of non-issue over and over again hoping to create some sort of controversy, some sort of scandal some sort of opening that the Democrats could capitalize on.

Story after story about the struggles and heroics of women, minorities, immigrants and homosexuals juxtaposed with story after story about the evils of white men, the evils of the military, the evils of Christianity, the evils of corporations and the evils of conservatives. Week after week of front-page headlines about the so-called abuse of murders and terrorists at Guantanamo Bay, yet barely a whisper about the videotaped beheadings of innocent civilians by these same types of people.

Television is no different. Watch the CBS Evening News sometime. Watch ABC News. Watch NBC News. Watch CNN, MSNBC or just about anything besides Fox. Watch them with an eye on maturity. Watch them with an eye on Relevancy and Proportion. Watch these broadcasts and tell me how any objective person could ever say these networks are not completely biased to left. The truth is they can't.

Not that this liberal bias on television is in any way limited to the news, mind you. The fact is that over the past decade, even the entertainment side of the business has gotten into the game. Ever watch Real Time with Bill Maher? How about ABC's Commander-in-Chief with Geena Davis as the President? What about any of the day-time talk shows or the nighttime comedy specials with Robin Williams, Whoopi Goldberg or practically any other comedian that could actually manage to get on television? All liberal. Then, on top of it all, you have cable stations like Sundance and Bravo broadcasting 24-hour propaganda like the West Wing, the Al Frankin show and twenty-different varieties of Queer Eye for the Straight Guy.

Now take a look at the film industry. Remember all the panic in the media when Mel Gibson was about to release *The Passion of the Christ*? One Christian movie in who knows how many decades and every liberal in the country goes ballistic. Now contrast this to all the praise Michael Moore gets for the vile propaganda he pumps out every few years. Contrast this to movies like *GI Jane* which are meant to "educate" us about the evils of the military. Contrast this to the movie that was just released vilifying Joe McCarthy. Contrast this to what you see each and every time you walk into a theater.

Magazines? Can you even name a general circulation conservative-oriented magazine? I can't. On the other hand, I can name Time, People, Newsweek, Harper's, Cosmopolitan and so forth. Want to know what their agendas are—just take look at the covers.

How about the financial engine of the media world, the advertising industry? Completely dominated by gays and liberals.

What about books? Walk into any bookstore and you immediately see dozens of books bashing Bush prominently displayed everywhere you look. And if you want to write one that doesn't? Good luck trying to find an agent.

Yes, every element of the American media is controlled by liberals, and they have no qualms whatsoever about abusing it every way they can. But what about the few pieces of it they can't control like Fox News or talk radio? Not surprisingly, in these cases, liberals do what they always do—attack, attack and attack. Want proof? Just get on the Internet and within minutes you'll have no trouble finding dozens of well-financed websites set up for the sole-purpose of undermining Fox News, Rush Limbaugh, the Savage Nation and anything else that doesn't fit the liberal agenda. While you're at it, take a minute to read up on the so-called Fairness doctrine—the liberal's ultimate weapon to finally silence the opinions of those they despise.

Infesting Academia

According to a recent study[27], 72% percent of professors at American colleges and universities describe themselves as liberals, while only 15% consider themselves conservative. Worse yet, at the more elite schools, the study found that 87% percent of faculty is liberal while only 13% percent are conservative. Knowing everything we already know about liberal behavior, that alone should tell us what to expect.

However, if you want to learn more, just take a look at college curriculums these days. Sure, they still offer courses on math, physics, engineering, history, law and finance. Yet, more and more, the catalogues are filled with all sorts of garbage meant to pollute the minds of those who actually think they are working toward getting some sort of meaningful education. Gay studies. Women's studies. Native-American. African-American. Anti-American. Anything and everything to separate people and to teach them to do nothing, yet to demand everything. To teach them activism, in other words—how to spit in the face of a police officer and get away with it. How to lie down in the middle of the street and block traffic. Who to call when you get arrested—and who to sue.

What about campus speech codes? Go ahead; say something that someone who isn't white, male or Christian might be offended by. If you're lucky, you may get away with only a few hours of sensitivity training; if not, you'll probably be expelled.

Interested in the ROTC at Harvard? Don't get your hopes up because it was banished back in 1969. What about Stanford? Same thing; banned in 1969.

---

27   *Politics and Professional Advancement Among College Faculty* by Stanley Rothman, Smith College, S. Robert Lichter, Center of Media and Public Affairs and Neil Nevitte, University of Toronto. The study is based on a survey of 1,643 full-time faculty members at 183 four-year schools.

What if you happen to be considering a career in the military after graduation? Might as well forget about it; most of the well-known schools have banned military recruiters from even stepping foot on their campuses.

Now what if a college student actually wants to hear what conservatives have to say on an issue or if they happen to be interested in some kind of diversity of opinion? Please; don't make me laugh. Not only are there barely any conservatives on college faculties these days, but more often than not, the administration will do everything they can to prevent them from even speaking there.

When it comes to academia, liberals certainly know how to play the game. Get 'em while they're young. Get them while they're impressionable. Get them while they still think you have something to offer. Get them before they have developed enough sense to see what is really going on. Get them before they realize that—despite all the propaganda you expose them to—that ultimately, there is only one thing destroying our society—one thing known as *liberalism*.

Bashing Capitalism

Liberals are always bashing capitalism. They bash corporations as evil. They bash businessmen as greedy. They bash oil companies, tobacco companies, fast-food companies and drug companies. They sue, they slander, they boycott and they extort. They do everything they possibly can to undermine the very companies that provide them and the rest of society with the goods and services we all take for granted every day of our lives.

So what, you say? Let them bash capitalism? Let them turn people against a free market? Let them tear these people down, undermine these companies and destroy these industries? Let them do what they want, right? Wrong.

As we discussed back in Chapter 2, not only is capitalism the absolute pinnacle of Good Competition, but it also serves as a transformative process that can turn egotistical desires (such as the desire for money or power) into products or services that ultimately improve the standard of living for everyone. As a result, by attacking capitalism, not only are liberals destroying the very engine of our society, but they are also killing the one thing that can actually turn people into productive members of that society.

But what the all of the inequality of capitalism; in particular, the argument liberals' always make about how much CEOs are paid? After all, liberals always moan about how these "stupid white men" (as Michael Moore calls them) are making one-hundred, two-hundred, three-hundred, whatever-hundred times what the average employee makes. What about that?

You know, that's a good question. To answer it, we simply turn our focus onto some of the people in Hollywood who are so quick to tell everyone about this particular imbalance in our society. Then we ask some questions about them. Questions like, how much does Sean Penn get for making a movie? Whoopi Goldberg? What about Julia Roberts? Tom Cruise? Susan Sarandon? Then we study the answer—which is that they get anywhere from $5 million to $25 million per film.

Now take a look at what the average moviegoer makes. Since the median income is around $35,000 per year, we can assume this is the also the case for those people going to the movies. If we do this, some simple math tells us that the liberal loudmouths in Hollywood are making anywhere from *150 to 750 times* what each member of the audience makes. Talk about inequality. Forget CEOs; if these people actually cared about what they were saying, the real focus would be on a salary cap in Hollywood.

Raging Stupidity

Some people are incredibly smart—I can handle that. In the same way, some people are incredibly stupid—I can handle that. But I have to admit, there is one type of person I'm not quite sure how to handle—those who are incredibly stupid, yet think they are incredibly smart. Fortunately, although I may not be able to stand this kind of person, at least I have a name for their behavior—I call it raging stupidity.

Raging as in screaming, yelling, throwing tirades, shoving their opinions down your throat and endlessly insisting on all sorts of things they could not even begin to understand. The type of people who can barely add, yet are somehow experts in finance and economics. The type of people who have never held a job a day in their lives, yet somehow know how to run everything around them so much better than everyone else. The type of people who have never once put their lives at risk, yet are so quick to shriek about any action ever taken by a police officer, a soldier or anyone else who runs that risk each and every time they put on a uniform.

The same people who don't know the first thing about nuclear energy, but scream about how bad it is. The same people who have no understanding whatsoever about the military, yet try to undermine it every day. The same people who not only contribute absolutely nothing to society, but who continuously take and take and take and then still DEMAND more and more and more and more. The same people who know nothing about the computer, semiconductor or any other industry, yet DEMAND the companies within them put more women and minorities on their Boards of Directors.

The same people who talk about freedom of speech, yet are constantly screaming about what you are absolutely not allowed say under any circumstances. The same people who throw tirades over any mishandling of a Koran or of a cartoon of Allah with a bomb in his turban, yet praise art exhibits of crucifixes dipped in urine just for fun.

The same people who cut you off in line, then turn around and scream in your face as if it were you who did something wrong. The same people who go to concerts to supposedly help the environment, but instead leave tons of trash scattered around once the music ends. The same people who majored in nothing during seven years of college which they didn't even pay for, then have the nerve to hold boycotts against companies who refuse to hire them for jobs they are completely incapable of doing.

The same type of people who attack others each and every day of their lives in every vile, racist, sexist, man-hating way possible, yet throw tirade after tirade if someone says one thing, tells one joke, sends one email or dares to deviate in even the most miniscule way from what they deem to be acceptable.

The same people who lie in the street and block traffic for hours on end. The same people who are so quick to attack those who have given them everything. The same people who have the nerve to call themselves liberals.

Sound Bites

In reality, there are an incredibly limited number of concepts that can be reduced down to a single word or sentence. Unfortunately, liberals always try to do this with everything. Why? Simple—sound bites are easy to remember, easy to repeat and almost impossible to argue with.

If someone cared about an issue, believed in the logic they used to reach their conclusion or wanted to take a constructive approach to solving a problem, they would have no problem in taking the time to explain their reasoning in a mature, rational and productive manner. However, we rarely see this from the Left. In fact it's usually just the opposite. To liberals, chanting *No Justice, No Peace* over and over again somehow justifies destroying millions of dollars of property, terrorizing an entire city and attacking innocent people. To liberals, this single sound bite completely undermines any effort to have a rational discussion on the issue of what really went on during the L.A. riots.

In the same way, throwing out the sound bites of *Separation of Church and State* and *this country was built on immigrants* immediately stops any discussion of why historical monuments should not to be torn down or any attempt to evaluate the differences between people who came here to contribute to the society vs. those who come here to leach off it.

Another form liberal sound bites often take is to exploit the use of highly descriptive positive words to describe themselves. After all, we all know that liberals are *liberal, progressive, open-minded, free-thinking and enlightened*.

Of course, since exploiting these high-impact positive words to describe themselves is so useful to them, why not use high-impact *negative* words to describe conservatives? Not surprisingly, this is just what they do. Therefore, according to liberals, conservatives are *uptight, racist, homophobic, sexist, bigoted, hate-mongers, war-mongers, jingoistic, fascistic, xenophobic, chauvinistic, batterers* and so on.

In the same way, when liberals practice institutional racism, it isn't discrimination at all—it's *affirmative action*. When they demand preferential treatment, it isn't because they want something for nothing; it's simply part of their struggle for *human rights, gay rights, women's rights, civil rights, equality and justice*.

Aren't words wonderful?

Superficial

Just as sound bites try to reduce complex issues down to a handful of catchy words, there is also another very common way in which liberals try to avoid any constructive approach to problem solving. That way is to forget about the actual details or reasons for something and focus only on the superficial.

War is bad! Of course it is—who could argue with that? Unfortunately, this superficial analysis tells us absolutely nothing about a particular situation and what we should do about. *Women make only 72 cents for every dollar a man does!* True—but the real question is "why." *Blacks don't do as well on the SATs as white people, so the tests must be biased!* Really? They *must* be biased? There is no other possible explanation?

Again and again we see these sorts of statements from liberals. Never any analysis. Never any thought. Never anything but a superficial description of a situation and a hyper-simplistic conclusion as to what the reasons for it really are. The same reasons that a child would come up with.

Endless Repetition

A fairly simple liberal strategy is to endlessly repeat the same word or conclusion over and over again. Of course, this has no constructive purpose whatsoever, but it does allow a liberal to accomplish two of their most cherished goals—to avoid any meaningful dialogue and to annoy other people.

In particular, one often used manifestation of this strategy (usually employed by some member of the media) is to repeatedly ask the same question over and over again as if it were somehow the most important issue of all time. By doing so, not only does a liberal get to attack someone under the guise of journalism, but at the same time, they can also manage to create a permanent link between the accusation and the person or institution they are so vehemently attacking. As a result, the bottom line is that regardless of what actually happened or how the situation may ultimately unfold, the stigma liberals create through endless repetition almost never goes away.

Labels

Make no mistake about it, liberals love labels. By putting a label on something—or someone—liberals are not only able to avoid any meaningful discussion of an issue, but they can also immediately create a permanent bias, blow something completely out of proportion, annoy, undermine, insult, defy and harass all at the same time. Worse yet, with only a single word, liberals can immediately take a person, action or situation and put everything even vaguely related to it in the same box as the worst-case scenario.

Don't ever stop a woman from destroying your property—if you do, you'll be labeled a *batter*. Don't go to church more than once a year—if you do, you'll be labeled a *Jesus Freak*. Don't even think about trying to protect your family from someone trying to break into your house—if you do, you'll be labeled a *gun nut*. Don't you dare expect a minority to ever be accountable for their actions—if you do, you'll be labeled a *racist*.

Thanks to the liberals, we now live in a society where words are more important than logic. Where saying something is more important than actually understanding it. Where thinking is a lost art. Where reasons are belittled as excuses and excuses are glorified as reasons. Where up is down, bad is good, left is right and right is always wrong.

Discredit

We all know the liberal's preferred form of debate is to make personal attacks against their opponents—to call them and everything they do every vile name they can come up with. However, a closely related, but slightly more subtle liberal strategy is to do everything they possibly can to discredit a person in the hopes that by smearing them in some way, no one would ever pay any attention to anything that person would ever have to say.

Although liberals run this smear campaign in a variety of ways, one of their favorites is to continually make accusations against a person which—instead of focusing on the issues being debated—their opponent now has to take the time to defend themselves against.

Liberals also try to discredit people by finding someone with an axe to grind—an old girlfriend, an ex-wife, a former employee and so forth—to come forward and say something especially negative about them. Yet another way liberals try to neutralize someone is by finding something in that person's distant past that they can keep pointing to over and over again to annoy, frustrate, slander or embarrass a person into silence or obscurity.

Of course, if a liberal really had anything meaningful to say, they would not need to rely on this strategy of trying to discredit their opponent with things that had nothing whatsoever to do with the issue. However, the fact that liberals do employ this strategy so often, speaks volumes about what they really have to offer.

Potshots

People take potshots out of sheer desperation—desperation to belittle the success of others, or desperation to hide their own lack of ideas or accomplishment. That explanation in itself, would account for why we hear them so often from the Left.

Basically, a potshot is a critical remark made in some sort of random manner against an easy target. And since potshots are so easy, they can be taken against just about anyone and anything. *Einstein? The guy couldn't even comb his hair. Responsibility? Yeah, right—if you want to be a robot. Putting a man on the moon? So what, if I had $10 billion, I could do that too.* In fact, when you step back and look at what is really being said, it becomes quite clear that potshots are nothing more than nuggets of immaturity. Unfortunately, liberals could care less about embarrassing themselves with that reality and will therefore never hesitate to take whatever potshot they can, however they can, whenever they can and as often as they can.

Interestingly though, of all the potshots liberals take, their favorite type seems to be the closing remark. Just listen to a liberal try to debate an issue. After they have been completely obliterated by a rational argument in accordance with the principles of Relevancy and Proportion, a liberal will still come back with some sort of asinine statement. Apparently, if they can just get away with calling you one last name, get in one last word or annoy you in some little way, they can at least feel like they have actually accomplished something.

False Attribution

Another common liberal tactic is to put words in your mouth—to take an innocent, logical or rational statement and immediately counter it with an incredibly hostile response to some sort of extreme statement, desperately implying that you said something you did not.

We've all been in situations where liberals have done this. Maybe it was at a restaurant where someone said something like, "You can't have different laws for different people." Immediately, some liberal at the other end of the table will fire back with a complete non-sequitur like, "Why do you think all gays should be killed!"

Another example would be where a conservative might point out the absurdity of affirmative action by saying something like, "I just read that Berkley was admitting black students with SAT scores as low 600." Immediately, the nearest liberal will shout out, "I can't believe you think all black people are stupid!"

The question of course, is why would liberals need to do this? Then again, the answer should be obvious by now—they clearly do not believe they could ever legitimately defend their point of view on the issue so they have to invent something that they can defend. Something that has absolutely nothing to do with what you actually said.

Out-of-Context

This strategy is basically the same as the previous one except here liberals' try to use a person's own words against them. Then, once they edit, filter or reconstruct your statement, they immediately switch gears and endlessly harp on your purported point-of-view in order to make it seem as though it were something it was not.

Liberals did this with Bill Bennett, claiming he wanted to abort all black babies. Liberals did this with Arnold Schwarzenegger, claiming he admired Adolf Hitler. Liberals even did this with Cat Stevens of all people, claiming he endorsed the killing of Salman Rushdie for writing *The Satanic Verses*.

Here again, we have a clear example of liberals not believing that they could ever legitimately defend their point of view, so once again they have to invent something they can defend. Something that— as always—has absolutely nothing to do with the issue.

Credit Where Credit Isn't Due

One of the most interesting tools liberals use to undermine our society is to try to take credit for things they had nothing whatsoever to do with. Not surprisingly, doing this allows them to get something for nothing (the primary goal of liberalism) as well as to deny others of the reward or recognition they deserve for their efforts (the secondary goal of liberalism).

Although there are numerous ways in which liberals employ this tool on daily a basis (just listen to feminists whine about something sometime), a good example would be with regard to the statue that was planned to honor the 343 firefighters killed during the attack on the World Trade Center.

Thanks to liberals, the $180,000 sculpture—based on the famous photograph of three firefighters raising the American flag on top of twenty feet of rubble—was suddenly changed from three white firefighters as in the actual picture, into one white, one black and one Hispanic.

Instead of simply having the statue reflect the reality of the original photograph and to have the names of all the firefighters killed that day inscribed on the base—*without any reference to ethnicity*—liberals chose to turn the whole situation into a racial issue. Why? Not to honor the black firefighters who were killed. Not to honor the Hispanic firefighters who were killed. Not to honor *any* of the firefighters who were killed. Liberal turned the situation into a racial issue in order to find another way to honor themselves. Another way to take credit for something that they had absolutely nothing whatsoever to do with.

Unnatural Selection

As we know, natural selection is the evolutionary process by which a species changes through the emergence of new traits which make it easier for that species to survive. Over time, those members who have these new traits are able to thrive, while those who do not eventually die out. In other words, natural selection is survival of the fittest.

When it comes to biology, liberals strongly support the concept of natural selection. Yet, for some reason—despite their apparent understanding this concept—all liberal policies, all liberal solutions and all liberal ideologies are in complete contradiction of the process of natural selection.

Everything liberals think, do and say is focused not on survival of the strongest, but on survival of the weakest—on *unnatural* selection. Dissect any liberal policy (affirmative action, immigration policy, welfare, diversity, lowering standards to get certain people into certain positions, catering to those who refuse to learn English, disciplining children, the military, anything having to do with any kind of responsibility and so on) and it becomes immediately obvious that all of them are based on the weaker and less intelligent having priority over those who are stronger and more intelligent.

Of course, this inverted reality should come as no surprise—after all, like everything else liberalism stands for, unnatural selection is just another form of Bad Competition.

Burden of Proof

Unless you happen to be a liberal, you should expect to be guilty until proven innocent. You should expect to be guilty of being a racist—unless you can prove your innocence. You should expect to be guilty of being a sexist—unless you can prove your innocence. You should expect to be guilty of being a homophobe—unless you can prove your innocence. You should expect to be guilty of being a war-monger—unless you can prove your innocence.

You should expect to be guilty of exploitation. You should expect to be guilty of greed. You should expect to be guilty of repression and you should expect to be guilty of hate. You should expect to be guilty of everything white people have ever done unless you happen to be lucky enough not be white. In that case however, unless you completely conform to the most vile of all liberal ideologies, you should expect to be guilty of being a sell-out.

Entropy

In the field of thermodynamics, the term entropy is generally used as a measure of the amount of disorder in a particular system. Not surprisingly, the natural tendency is for this disorder to continue to increase unless a certain amount of work is done to stop it. Interestingly, the same is true of a society; unless a huge amount of effort is put into maintaining order, we should expect it to ultimately collapse into complete anarchy.

Unfortunately, like spoiled children, liberals are always there to make a mess of everything. Lies, slander, propaganda and hate. Endless accusations that need to be addressed. Endless protests, riots, sabotage and criticism. More and more noise. More and more problems. More and more issues that take time up time, burn through resources and destroy the will of the people trying to maintain that order.

Asinine laws. Raging stupidly. Entitlements. Taking and taking, complaining and complaining, attacking and attacking until everywhere you look there is another mess to be cleaned up, another fire to be put out, another thousand rumors to be squelched and another million frivolous lawsuits to deal with.

Over time, it becomes impossible to sustain this sort of system. Eventually, no matter how much effort responsible people put in to maintaining order, there is just not enough to go around. Eventually, the system fails. Eventually, the society collapses. Eventually, liberals get exactly what it is they want—to bring it all down, man.

Feigning Confusion

All too often, in a discussion, argument or debate, a liberal will look at the other person and act as if they just made the most asinine statement of all time. The liberal seems completely confused by what was just said, implying that it was so incredibly stupid they must surely have missed something.

I've got news for you—don't buy it. Don't buy it because liberals love feigning confusion. Liberals love to employ what I call the *sucker strategy*—and guess who the sucker is. You. The sucker conservative who sits there for hour after hour trying to explain and re-explain something to someone who will continue to pretend they don't understand it just because they have absolutely no idea whatsoever as to how to counter it.

Victimization

One of the most powerful tools in the liberal arsenal is that of being a victim—or at least appearing to be. Victims are sympathetic. Victims have been wronged in some way. Victims deserve compensation, they deserve protection and they deserve justice. Victims are the perfect way for liberals to move the discussion on any issue away from logic, rationality, cause, effect and objectiveness and replace them with emotion, sympathy, bias and hatred.

Liberals hold nothing back when it comes to trying to make themselves or the people they exploit look like victims. In return, they get huge paydays in terms of cash settlements, in terms of special programs, in terms of exemptions from responsibility and in terms of more opportunities for them to undermine the society that others have worked so hard to create.

Invent-A-Crime

An increasingly prevalent tool liberals have used to undermine our society is to invent new kinds of crimes and then find ways to make sure as many people as possible are guilty of them. The process works as follows:

1. Liberals turn speech, thought, responsibly, objectivity or anything else they are incapable of dealing with in a rational way into some sort of crime;

2. They come up with a catchy, high impact name (e.g. sexual harassment, domestic violence, hate speech, hostile work environment, homophobia and so forth) for the crime;

3. They endlessly harp on the evils of the crime;

4. They cast as wide a net as possible in order to make any person who does not cater to their agenda guilty of the crime; and

5. They find a way to justify the harshest penalties possible for those who commit these crimes including imprisonment, asset seizures, prosecution by the state even when the purported victim refuses to press charges, loss of rights, public humiliation and any other way they can come up with to ostracize these individuals in order to exclude them and their opinions from the rest of society.

A perfect example of how liberals employ this strategy would be the situation in April, 2006 where Scott Savage—a librarian at

Ohio State University—was slapped with a sexual harassment charge for recommending that some conservative books be included in the school curriculum. By simply making this recommendation, Savage was put under investigation by the Office of Human Resources after three professors filed discrimination and harassment complaints against him. The professors claimed the books he suggested made them feel "unsafe."

Name Calling

Without a doubt, there is no tool or methodology used more often by liberals than that of calling other people names. Politicians do it. Journalists do it. Protestors do it. Political commentators, college professors, friends, relatives, black, white, gay, straight or whatever.

With very few exceptions, no matter who they are or what the issue is, the most common way for a liberal to deal with any situation is to call other people names. Of course, you certainly didn't need me to tell you this, but for the sake of completeness, I've decided to include it anyway.

Lies

It should be more than obvious by this point that practically everything the Left says is a complete and utter lie. Every statistic is a lie. Every guise is a lie. Every accusation is a lie. Every assumption is a lie. Every agenda is a lie. Every mention of any sort of Right-Wing conspiracy is nothing but a lie.

Every policy is a lie. Every justification is a lie. Every claim of caring or compassion or equality or justice—with the exception of those made by an incredibly small and constantly shrinking minority of liberals who have yet to realize what has happened to their cherished ideology over the past thirty years—is nothing but another lie. Make no mistake about it; just about everything liberals ever say on any social or political issue is nothing but one big lie.

Fortunately, the whole point of this book has been to expose the tools and methodologies liberals use to obscure and perpetuate these lies. As long as you remember them, their lies will always be obvious.

Undermine

Undermine. The last tool in our discussion of how liberals are destroying our society. Then again, looking back on the past two-hundred pages, we should realize that undermining is not a tool at all—undermining is *the* tool.

Undermining is what liberals do in each and every situation they involve themselves in. Undermining is what liberals live for. Undermining is what ties together all of the other tools we've discussed. If you take nothing else away from reading this book, remember this one thing—*undermining* is what modern-day liberalism is all about.

Afterword

One of the most frustrating experiences any rational person could ever have is to listen to liberals try to justify their position on any sort of social or political issue. However, now that we have had the chance to explore their actions, statements and behaviors from a completely different perspective than what is typically offered by other forms of political analysis, we should have no problem whatsoever in seeing just how predictable—and how destructive—everything they do really is.

Moreover, based on the insights offered by this remarkably high level of predictability, we have been able to construct a new framework for segmenting and isolating these statements, actions and behaviors into the most objective and discrete elements possible and have gone through countless examples of just how these tools and methodologies manifest themselves over and over again throughout our society. As a result of this analysis, the ultimate goal of this book—to ensure rational people are able to immediately recognize and understand the true nature of these liberal shenanigans whenever they see them—comes down to nothing more than a little bit of practice.

As painful as it may be, take the time to listen to what your liberal friends, relatives, neighbors or co-workers may say with regard to social and political issues. Listen as they speak. Listen to how they speak. Listen to the words they use and listen as they endlessly employ—consciously or unconsciously—three, four, five or more of the tools and methodologies discussed in this book in each and every argument they try to make.

Now do the same thing with liberal politicians, activists and members of the mainstream media. Listen to what they say and how they say it. Then take a minute to break down every one of their statements, speeches or sound bites into the elements we've discussed. With a little practice, it should become painfully obvious which of the specific tools or methodologies are being used at any given time as they try to justify, rationalize or defend any of their indefensible positions, policies or agendas.

Sure, sometimes their arguments are passionate and on rare occasion they may even have some trace of merit, but the key problem—as explored in the chapter on Relevancy and Proportion—is that just about everything they say has absolutely nothing to do with the issue. But now, no matter what they do or say, at least we know exactly why they're doing it—even if they don't.

When a liberal make all sorts of wild accusations about sexism or racial inequality, we know they are relying on a set of Implicit Assumptions as they try desperately to Promote and Exploit Divisiveness. When they talk about the need for Asymmetry and Bad Competition as represented by schemes like affirmative action or Guises like diversity, hate crimes or empowerment, we immediately know they are necessarily invoking the confused logic of Groupdividual.

When they talk about the horror of everything wrong in any situation while conveniently ignoring the overwhelming number of things that are right, we understand how important it is for them to be Negative. And when they throw out all sorts of numbers to try to make their case, we can be sure that they are relying on nothing more than the power of Statistical Manipulations.

Make no mistake about it, the tools and methodologies explored in this book have permeated every element of our society and as a result, I have little doubt that over the next forty to fifty years, the United States as we know it will cease to exist. The name may not change, the borders may stay the same, but one thing is certain—it will no longer be the same country it was. And unless enough people begin to understand just how liberalism really operates, there is no chance whatsoever that we will ever be able to do anything to stop it.

I sincerely hope the analyses offered within this book can help people begin to develop that understanding.

APPENDIX A

The Arithmetic of Importance

Here we briefly revisit our discussion on Relevancy and Proportion from Chapter 4 in order to introduce a more precise definition of the concept of *importance*. Although this discussion is really meant for people who enjoy math, the fact that it is relatively straightforward means that most people should not have much of a problem following it if they have an interest in doing so.

As was the case in Chapter 4, the first step to creating this new definition is to realize that in any meaningful discussion or analysis, there are only two things that really matter—relevancy and proportion. Relevancy is the concept of applicability—to what extent does a particular point or statement actually matter to the issue being discussed? Proportion, on the other hand, is how much an issue matters in comparison to the others that need to be considered.

The second step in creating our new definition is to realize that we should be able to quantify both relevancy and proportion reasonably well as long as we apply some level of objectivity to the analysis. Clearly in any situation, the relevancy of something may range from absolutely critical (we define this to mean a relevancy of 10) to one which has no applicability whatsoever (which we define as a relevancy of 0).

Similarly, proportion may also range from 0 to 10 depending on how important an issue is in comparison to the others that need to be considered. Although a particular statement may be absolutely true and completely relevant, when measured against other issues, the value of that particular point may be of little consequence.

Now that we have these two key pieces in place, we can go ahead and formulate our new definition; the only thing we need to know at this point is how much each of these elements really matter. Along those lines, we can make a fairly simple assumption, that assumption being that they both matter in the exact same amount.

That being the case, the best way to define importance in any given situation would be to take the average of these two quantities. However, in order to come up with the most usable definition we possibly can, the average we take will not be to add relevancy and proportion and divide by two (the arithmetic mean); rather it will be to take what is known as the *geometric mean*. As such, we can now propose the following definition: Importance = square-root of (Relevancy X Proportion). In simpler terms, $I = \sqrt{R \times P}$.

One thing we can immediately see from this definition is that if a statement has an extremely high relevancy (let's say a 10) along with an extremely high proportion (another 10), then the importance of that particular statement is also a 10 (ten times ten is one-hundred, the square-root of which is also ten). At the same time, we can immediately see that if something has a relevancy of 10 but a proportion of 0 (for example, the case where one instance out of a thousand actually supports the statement being made), then the importance of that statement is also 0 (since any number multiplied by zero is zero).

Defining importance in this way gives us a powerful tool to understand the best way to think about something, as well as a way to immediately discredit any sort of nonsensical argument. The best part of all of this however, is that in most cases—such as those discussed in Chapter 4—we won't even have to go through the math. Instead, we simply take a moment to independently analyze the relevancy and proportion of each statement: when coming from a liberal, one or the other will usually be so low that the insignificance of it will be immediately obvious—and you can now tell them exactly why.

For completeness, we should briefly discuss what the various levels of importance actually mean. When objective values for relevancy and proportion are used in our definition, the importance of any statement will fall into the range of 0 - 10. When, in a specific instance, the importance falls between 0 - 2.0, we can safely say the statement is completely unimportant; in other words, noise. Likewise, we can define a range of 2.1 - 4.0 to mean a statement is not of meaningful importance; a range of 4.1 - 6.0 to be somewhat important; a range of 6.1 - 8.0 as very important and a range of 8.1 - 10 to be incredibly important.

By using this simple criteria, any objective person will find that over and over again, the importance of most liberal arguments tend to fall into the range 0 - 2.0 (i.e. noise) whereas most (though not all) conservative and libertarian arguments tend to come out at a 7+.

Index

Other Books By Richard Mgrdechian:

Richard Mgrdechian may be reached via email at:
author@howtheleftwaswon.com.

About the Author

Richard Mgrdechian holds a Bachelor's Degree in Electrical Engineering from the California Institute of Technology, along with an MBA from Columbia University. His background includes positions as a NASA engineer, investment banker, and high-tech entrepreneur and CEO. In addition to his current book, *How The Left Was Won*, he is the author of the Prometheus Award nominated social-commentary, *3000 Years*.

Printed in the United States
60293LVS00004B/30